Guide to Mental Health for Families and Carers of People with Intellectual Disabilities

of related interest

Mental Illness
A Handbook for Carers
Edited by Rosalind Ramsay, Claire Gerada, Sarah Mars and George Szmukler
ISBN 1 85302 934 3

Women with Intellectual Disabilities
Finding a Place in the World
Edited by Rannveig Traustadottir and Kelley Johnson
ISBN 1 85302 846 0

Living with Genetic Syndromes Asssociated with Intellectual Disability
Marga Hogenboom
ISBN 1 85302 984 X

Working with People with Learning Disabilities
Theory and Practice
David Thomas and Honor Woods
ISBN 1 85302 973 4

Lifemaps of People with Learning Disabilities
Barry Gray and Geoff Ridden
ISBN 1 85302 690 5

A Multidisciplinary Handbook of Child and Adolescent Mental Health
for Front-line Professionals
Nisha Dogra, Andrew Parkin, Fiona Gale and Clay Frake
ISBN 1 85302 929 7

Guide to Mental Health for Families and Carers of People with Intellectual Disabilities

Geraldine Holt, Anastasia Gratsa, Nick Bouras,
Theresa Joyce, Mary Jane Spiller and
Steve Hardy

Jessica Kingsley Publishers
London and Philadelphia

The right of Geraldine Holt, Anastasia Gratsa and Nick Bouras to be identified as authors of this work has been asserted by them in accordance with the Copyright, Designs and Patents Act 1988.

First published in the United Kingdom in 2004
by Jessica Kingsley Publishers
116 Pentonville Road
London N1 9JB, England
and
400 Market Street, Suite 400
Philadelphia, PA 19106, USA

www.jkp.com

Library of Congress Cataloging in Publication Data
A CIP catalog record for this book is available from the Library of Congress

British Library Cataloguing in Publication Data
A CIP catalogue record for this book is available from the British Library

ISBN 1 84310 277 3

Printed and Bound in Great Britain by
Athenaeum Press, Gateshead, Tyne and Wear

Contents

Acknowledgements

We are grateful to the Steering Group members who helped in the preparation of this book: Hazel Morgan, Brian McGinnis, Anna Eliatamby and Shirley Linden. Our gratitude goes also to Anne Faulkner, Amy Cowley and Helen Wooding for their support and advice.

A special thanks to all the carers who took part in this project.

This project has been supported by a generous grant from the Guy's and St Thomas' Charitable Foundation.

Finding Your Way
Around this Guide

Chapter 1: General information regarding mental health problems

Look here to find information on:

- Signs and symptoms of the most common mental health problems, including psychotic symptoms such as delusions and hallucinations in people with intellectual disabilities

- Challenging behaviour

- How mental health problems affect people and self-awareness

- What causes mental health problems: biological, psychological and social factors

- Diagnosis and treatment of mental health problems in intellectual disabilities: mental health assessments; supporting the person and preparing information for the assessment; physical examination; health screening

- General steps you can take to help the person you care for during the assessment period and afterwards

- How to deal with difficult behaviours such as sleeping or withdrawing a lot of the time; inactivity and not feeling like doing anything; aggressive behaviour; not taking prescribed medication

- General resources for people with intellectual disabilities and mental health problems and their carers

- Services, getting emotional support, respite, self-help groups for the person you care for and support for you

Chapter 2: Mental health problems

Look here to find information on the most common mental health problems in people with intellectual disabilities: what they are (e.g. symptoms), diagnosis and what to do to help the person you care for. This chapter also contains useful resources (e.g. organizations that provide information on different mental health problems and self-help groups) concerning:

- Affective disorders: depression, manic depression, mania
- Schizophrenia
- Anxiety disorders: phobia, panic disorder, obsessive compulsive disorder, post-traumatic stress disorder and generalized anxiety disorder
- Adjustment disorders and acute stress reaction
- Dementia, Alzheimer's disease
- Eating disorders: pica, rumination, regurgitation, excessive spitting, food faddiness, anorexia, bulimia
- Substance misuse: illegal substances, drugs and alcohol
- Personality disorders

Chapter 3: Services for people with intellectual disabilities and mental health problems

Look here to find information on:

- UK Government Policy on Services such as 'Valuing People', National Service Framework for Mental Health, Care Programme Approach, Health Action Plans
- Community Learning Disabilities Services, Specialist Mental Health in Learning Disabilities Services, In-Patient Services, Primary Care Services such as GPs and their role
- Community Mental Health Teams, Crisis Resolution/Home Treatment Teams, Assertive Outreach Teams, Community Learning Disabilities Teams, Multi-Disciplinary Teams

- Ways you can help services
- Other services such as Direct Payments, Person-Centred Planning, Advocacy, Respite Services or short-term breaks, Day and Employment Services, Housing and planning for the future
- Useful resources and organizations that provide information and support in the areas listed above

Chapter 4: Therapeutic interventions

Look in here to find information on:

- What therapeutic interventions are
- Biological therapies and medication; side effects; what information you should get from the doctor or nurse; how the medication would be monitored; medication for depression, manic depression, schizophrenia, anxiety, dementia
- Psychological therapies including cognitive behavioural therapy, psychodynamic psychotherapy, counselling, family therapy, behaviour therapy and skills training methods, the ABC approach, relaxation training and also dramatherapy, art therapy, music therapy
- Social therapies
- Helping the person you care for to communicate
- How you can support the person with interventions

Chapter 5: Challenging behaviour

Look in here to find information on:

- Explanations of difficult or challenging behaviour and causes
- Functional analysis and assessment process, reinforced behaviour and triggers

- De-escalation and redirection strategies and different kinds of therapeutic interventions

- Monitoring of interventions

- Consent

Chapter 6: Law, policy and ethical issues

Look in here to find information on:

- Confidentiality and 'best interests'

- What it means to 'give consent' and capacity to consent

- The Mental Health Act (1983)

- The Human Rights Act (2000)

- The Disability Discrimination Act (1995)

- Physical interventions as defined by the British Institute of Learning Disabilities (BILD), policy and ethical framework

- Patient forums

- Resources and contact details of different organizations that provide information and deal with legal issues

Chapter 7: Autism

Look in here to find information on:

- The core features of autism including impairment in three main areas

- What causes autism

- Language in social communication, echolalia, symbolic or imaginative play

- 'Autistic spectrum disorders' and Asperger's syndrome

- The process of multi-disciplinary assessment and medical assessment

- Observing the person's behaviour and interaction with others

- Rituals and stereotyped behaviours, compulsive actions, unusual dietary habits, sleep disturbance, abnormalities of mood, self-injurious behaviour, lack of response to pain, heightened sensitivity to sound, preoccupation with tactile stimulation

- What may happen in the long term

- Additional emotional and behavioural problems: anti-social behaviour, disruptive behaviour, anxiety, depression, attention deficit hyperactivity disorder

- Therapeutic interventions for autism

- How you can help the person you care for

- Resources and contact details of organizations that deal with autism

Chapter 8: Epilepsy

Look in here to find information on:

- What epilepsy is, 'non-convulsive seizures', generalized seizures, partial seizures (simple or complex), triggers of seizures, tonic-clonic (grand mal), myoclonic, atonic, and absence (petit mal)

- How common epilepsy is

- Epilepsy in people with Down syndrome

- Epilepsy and the mental processes of knowing and thinking

- Assessment and diagnosis

- Therapeutic interventions such as medication, blood tests, side effects and psychosocial interventions

- How you can help the person you care for with the assessment and after the assessment

- Resources and contact details of organizations that specialize in epilepsy

Chapter 9: Carers' needs and support

Look in here to find information on:

- Practical and emotional support for carers
- Definitions of who is a carer
- The Carers (Recognition and Services) Act (1995)
- What services carers should expect
- Using the internet and libraries
- National Service Framework for Mental Health (1999)
- The Carers Act (1996)
- What a Carer Assessment is and what to expect
- Caring for Carers (1999), also known as the National Carers Strategy
- Carers and employment
- What carers can do to help themselves
- Resources, useful contacts and voluntary organizations for carers

What is this Guide for?

Mary Jane Spiller

This is a Guide to mental health for families and carers of adults who have intellectual disabilities.

Adults with intellectual disabilities are more vulnerable to mental health problems than the general population. Also, mental health problems can go undetected in an adult with intellectual disabilities and so remain untreated.

For these reasons this Guide aims to provide carers and family members with information about a wide range of mental health issues in an accessible and easy-to-read way.

Who is this Guide for and what is it about?

If you are caring for an adult with intellectual disabilities and you want to know more about mental health issues then this Guide is for you. As a carer for someone with intellectual disabilities it can be very important for you to be able to find out information about a range of mental health issues. This is because people with intellectual disabilities are more vulnerable to mental health problems than the general population. People with intellectual disabilities can develop the same mental health problems as anyone else and, although many of the signs and symptoms will be the same, some can be very different. Also, some of the symptoms that would signal a problem in someone without intellectual disabilities might be dismissed as simply being a part of the intellectual disability. Consequently, not only are people with intellectual disabilities more at risk of developing a mental health problem, but also these problems can often go undetected or unrecognized for a long time. This means that they remain untreated, making life more difficult and challenging for yourself, the person you care for, and others around.

There is lots of information already available about caring for someone with a mental health problem. However, it is much more difficult to find information specifically written about caring for someone with intellectual disabilities who also has a mental health problem. This Guide has been written to provide you with this. It provides a wide range of information about many different mental health issues for a person with intellectual disabilities, and about caring for someone with intellectual disabilities who develops a mental health problem. We hope that all of this will make the process of getting help and assistance much easier, and also help you to understand the mental health problem by:

- Knowing about the different signs and symptoms of a mental health problem and helping you to understand any unusual or out-of-character behaviour

- Knowing what to do if you suspect the person you care for has a mental health problem

- Knowing about the sorts of things you can do to help

A general overview of mental health problems is presented in Chapter 1, providing a good understanding of mental health issues specifically for people with intellectual disabilities. The different ways mental health problems can affect someone's life or behaviour are presented, along with the many different causes of mental health problems. This chapter also describes what happens if you think the person you care for might have a mental health problem – what is known as the 'Mental Health Assessment'. Advice is given for you as a carer about what you will need to do for this assessment, and how you can support the person you care for. This is a very general introduction to mental health problems, and if you want further information there is a list of people you can contact to find out more at the end of the chapter.

More detailed information about specific mental health problems for people with intellectual disabilities is provided in Chapter 2. This chapter has sections that describe the different mental health problems, their signs and symptoms, and how these can be treated. These sections also include advice for you about what you can do to help the person you care for, and each section has a list of people you can contact for more detailed information about that specific problem.

In Chapter 3, this Guide provides you with information about the kinds of services the person you care for may be able to access, and the types of professionals you might meet. It lists questions these professionals might ask you, and information you may need to provide. It also suggests questions you might want to ask when you meet these professionals. This chapter's main focus is on current services available for people who have intellectual disabilities and additional mental health needs in England and Wales, and the government policies around these services. The recent White Paper 'Valuing People: A New Strategy for Learning Disability for the Twenty-First Century' and the National Service Framework for Mental Health are central to this chapter.

If the person you care for has a mental health problem the health professionals involved may suggest a way of helping the person to cope with the illness, or to make them better, which can be called a therapeutic intervention. Chapter 4 outlines the different kinds of therapeutic interventions that might be suggested for someone with intellectual disabilities and additional mental health problems. These can include medication, psychological therapies, and techniques for managing someone's behaviour (a full description of each of these and what they involve is given in the chapter). For a carer for someone who might one day have one of these interventions as a part of their care plan or treatment this chapter is especially useful. It is important for you to understand the reasons for using the different interventions, and what they each involve. Your support, and sometimes your involvement, in interventions can be very helpful. You might also need to help explain them to the person you care for. Contact details are given at the end of the chapter for people you can get further information from, including leaflets written especially for people with intellectual disabilities.

An important aspect included in this mental health guide for people with intellectual disabilities is the chapter on challenging behaviour (Chapter 5). Although challenging behaviour is not an illness, it is a type of behaviour that can be associated with mental (and physical) illness, and it is a problem faced by many carers of adults with intellectual disabilities. This chapter describes what challenging behaviour is, and offers some possible explanations. It also describes the type of assessment that might be used to work out the cause of, or reason for, an individual's challenging behaviour. From this professionals can help the individual to learn more appropriate and acceptable ways of letting others know what they want, or what they are feeling. Your support with this can be central to its success.

Chapter 6 provides the key details of the legal and ethical issues concerning mental health and intellectual disabilities. In this chapter important ethical issues are outlined that relate to the mental health care of the person you care for, such as the issues of confidentiality and consent. Both of these are of particular importance when caring for someone with intellectual disabilities, and situations can often arise when you need to know a bit about them. This chapter also gives you an overview of significant documents such as the Mental Health Act, the Human Rights Act, and the Disability Discrimination Act, in order to help you know more about the legal rights of the person you care for. You can get more detailed information about these legal issues from many of the organizations listed at the end of the chapter.

Chapters 7 and 8 provide information about autism and epilepsy. Neither of these are mental health problems, but there are high rates of people with intellectual disabilities who have one or even both of them. Also, if someone has either autism or epilepsy they are more vulnerable to mental health problems. Each chapter provides an overview of what each of the conditions are, how they can affect people, how they might be assessed, and the therapeutic interventions that can be used. The chapters also suggest possible ways that you can help the person you care for if they are diagnosed with either of these conditions. Contact details are also provided at the end of each chapter for organizations that can give you more detailed information, and provide support and advice.

Chapter 9 has been written specifically for you, as a carer for someone with intellectual disabilities. Although as a carer you may have little time to think about your own health needs, looking after your own physical and emotional health is very important. This chapter outlines the kinds of services that should be accessible to you, and the support you should receive. It also provides contact details for a vast number of organizations that are there to offer you support, advice and information, covering a wide range of topics. Over a quarter of a million adults become a carer in any one year, and these agencies and organizations have been set up, usually by other carers, to help share knowledge, experience and skills.

How can you use the Guide?

As described already, each chapter in this Guide gives you information about an important mental health issue for people with intellectual disabilities. It may be that some of these chapters are not relevant to you and the person you care for at this time. However, the information provided in these chapters may be useful to you in years to come. This Guide has been written in such a way that you can use it to look up the relevant information as and when you need it. To make it easier to find where things are discussed there is a summary of the key messages of each issue at the start of the chapters. At the end of the Guide there is an explanation of different words and phrases used (the Glossary). This section can also be used as a quick and easy reference point for any words or phrases to do with mental health that you are uncertain of, or which you might come across in the future.

Chapter 1 provides a general overview to mental health problems for people with intellectual disabilities and it is useful to read this chapter first before reading any of the other sections. This chapter should make the sections in the other chapters easier to understand.

Chapter 2 provides specific information about a range of different mental health problems, and suggests ways that you can help the person you care for if they are diagnosed as having one of these. These suggestions are made to help you cope with certain behaviours associated with mental health problems. When reading these it is important to remember that every person is different and everyone's circumstances are different. You may like to try some suggestions but if these do not work for you make sure you consult with the person's mental health professional to find other ways that may work instead. Perhaps the particular suggestion needs to be changed slightly in order to work better.

How was the Guide written?

The contents of this Guide were decided on by talking to people like you, who care for someone with intellectual disabilities and additional mental health problems. They told us what they would find useful in a Guide like this, and how they wanted to be able to use it. We also spoke to people with intellectual disabilities who use mental health services to find out what they wanted their carers to know about, and what they thought should be in the Guide.

We hope this Guide is of use to you and your family in finding out about mental health issues for people with intellectual disabilities. We hope this is a useful mental health guide, and that it provides enough information for you about the wide range of topics covered, and about other organizations you can contact if you need more detailed information about a specific issue. This is an area of health and social care that is slowly starting to receive the recognition it deserves, and as more services are made available for people with intellectual disabilities, this will continue to grow. People are also becoming increasingly aware of the crucial role carers play in providing support, not just for the person they care for, but for other carers and their local community as a whole. We hope this Guide helps to highlight the importance of carers, not only in the value of the role they play in caring, but also in the wealth of their knowledge and experience, and how this can help other carers and professionals, as it has done with the development of this Guide.

Chapter 1

General Information Regarding Mental Health Problems

Geraldine Holt, Steve Hardy and Anastasia Gratsa

Key messages from this chapter
Introduction
Mental health problems
How do mental health problems affect people?
What causes mental health problems?
Mental health assessment
General advice to you as a carer
How to deal with difficult behaviours
Health screening
Resources

Key messages from this chapter

- People with intellectual disabilities can develop the same mental health problems as anyone else.
- People with intellectual disabilities are more at risk of developing mental health problems due to a number of biological, psychological and social vulnerability factors.

---

continued…

...continued

- People with mild intellectual disabilities show similar signs and symptoms of mental health problems to the rest of the population, but they may have difficulty in expressing their emotions and thoughts.
- People with severe intellectual disabilities tend to show the signs and symptoms of a mental health problem through changes in their behaviour.
- Mental health assessments should be multi-disciplinary, involving different health and social care professionals.
- Carers are able to assist in the assessment process by providing information about the person, what the problem is and any changes that have happened.
- Mental health problems can be really distressing for the person and the people who care for him or her.
- There are a number of things that you might be able to do to help and support the person who has a mental health problem in assessment, relapse prevention and treatment.
- It is important for you to seek information, support and advice for yourself as well as for the person you care for (see also Chapter 9).

Introduction

Mental health problems can affect people with learning disabilities[1] just like anyone else; in fact they are more vulnerable to developing them. It can sometimes be difficult to recognize mental health problems in people with intellectual disabilities. This is due to many reasons including limited communication skills and carers having a lack of experience in the area.

The information in this chapter is intended to help you understand and recognize the basic signs and symptoms of the most common mental health problems. It also discusses some of the causes of mental health problems and how they are assessed.

Information about the therapeutic interventions used for these mental health problems is given in Chapter 4.

Mental health problems

A mental health problem means that people experience changes in:

- The way they think and understand the world around them
- The way they behave
- The emotions and feelings they have

These changes will usually have some impact on the way the person deals with day-to-day life. Sometimes the impact is very great (ongoing problems with repeated relapse episodes) and then we talk about mental illness.

How do mental health problems affect people?

Mental health problems can affect people in many different ways. Areas of a person's life that can be affected by a mental health problem include:

- Biological changes in sleep pattern, appetite and weight
- Reduction or loss of skills, inability to learn new skills
- Increase in ritualistic movements, such as hand flapping and body rocking
- Increase in minor physical complaints
- Communication (verbal and non-verbal)
- Social withdrawal or becoming over-friendly and familiar, even with complete strangers
- Energy and activity levels
- Physical appearance
- Low, high or irritable mood
- Difficulties with memory
- Adaptation to new environments and situations
- Reduced concentration
- Conflict in relationships

Psychotic symptoms

In some severe mental health problems the person can experience psychotic symptoms. This means the person loses touch with reality. These symptoms include hallucinations and delusions. Psychotic symptoms can occur in schizophrenia, severe depression, bipolar affective disorder, delirium and dementia.

HALLUCINATIONS

This is when a person has an experience through one of their senses, which is not happening. It is imaginary. They can happen in every sense. Examples include:

- Hearing voices when no one else can

- Smelling odours when no one else can

- Seeing things that are not really there

- Feeling things on your skin when nothing is there

- Experiencing strange tastes without eating anything

DELUSIONS

These are false beliefs and it is generally very difficult, if not impossible, to change the person's mind about their belief. The beliefs tend to be quite strange, often bizarre and out of character. Delusions can be persecutory, for example people might think spies are following them or that everybody is out to get him or her. They can also be grandiose, for example believing they are related to the royal family or that they have super powers and can fly.

When assessing the possibility of psychotic symptoms being present, professionals need to consider the person's cultural and social background. This is because in other parts of the world people may hold different values and beliefs that could appear abnormal in another country. These could be mistaken for psychotic symptoms.

People with intellectual disabilities can experience psychotic symptoms but they tend to be simple and less complex than in a person of average intelligence. For example someone with intellectual disabilities who is having grandiose delusions might believe that he is a qualified electrician when he is not.

Challenging behaviour

This includes behaviours such as aggression, self-injury and being anti-social. They can occur for many different reasons such as communicating the need for attention, to escape from stressful situations or relieve boredom. However, sometimes challenging behaviour can happen because of mental health problems. This is generally where the behaviour is new or starts happening more often.

Picking up on mental health problems

People with mild intellectual disabilities will generally show the same signs and symptoms as the rest of the population, but they may need help to describe these. It is more difficult for people with severe intellectual disabilities as some of them have great difficulty in communicating in words. We may have to rely on changes in behaviour to indicate if they have a mental health problem.

What causes mental health problems?

We know very little about the causes of mental health problems compared to what is known about physical health problems. It is an area that causes much discussion among professionals and is constantly being researched.

It is generally believed that it is not just one factor that causes someone to develop a mental health problem, but a combination of factors. These factors can be broken down into **biological**, **psychological** and **social** factors. People with intellectual disabilities are more likely to be affected by these vulnerability factors (be more vulnerable/at risk) by virtue of their disability.

Many of us will have or will encounter these vulnerability factors throughout our lives. It just means that we are more vulnerable because of them. It does not definitely mean that we will develop a mental health problem.

Biological factors
BRAIN CHEMICALS

There are many chemicals in the brain that carry different messages from brain cell to brain cell. For example the chemical 'serotonin' carries messages about your mood. It is suggested that if we have too little 'serotonin' going between brain cells then we are more likely to become depressed. Another chemical called 'dopamine' carries messages about the way we see the world around us. If we have too much 'dopamine' being passed across brain cells then we are more likely to have psychotic symptoms as in schizophrenia.

RUNNING IN THE FAMILY

It has been found that some types of mental health problems can run in families. However, just because a relative has a mental health problem it does not mean that you will definitely develop it as well; there is just a slightly increased risk. It should also be remembered that there are other factors that will have a great impact on whether or not someone develops a mental health problem.

SENSORY IMPAIRMENTS

People with intellectual disabilities are more likely to experience sensory loss such as poor hearing and vision. People with sensory impairments are more vulnerable to mental health problems, especially those with hearing loss. Sensory impairments can be very difficult to pick up, especially in people with severe and profound intellectual disabilities. This will result in extra stress on the person.

CHRONIC PHYSICAL DISABILITY

People with chronic physical disability are more vulnerable to depression. There are higher rates of physical disability in people with intellectual disabilities.

PHYSICAL HEALTH PROBLEMS

People with intellectual disabilities are more likely to develop physical health problems. They are also less likely to seek medical advice about these problems sometimes due to a lack of understanding and communication difficulties.

DRUG AND ALCOHOL ABUSE

People who abuse drugs and alcohol are more at risk of developing mental health problems.

Psychological factors
LIFE EVENTS

There are events throughout life that may cause us stress. Such events include the death of a family member or close friend, unemployment, a relationship ending. It has been found that in some cases such life events can make us vulnerable to developing a mental health problem.

There are other life events that may affect people with intellectual disabilities. These include:

- Changes in the family home, such as a brother or sister moving out
- Key worker, social worker or outreach worker leaving their job
- Going into hospital
- Any type of assault or abuse

These can be made even more difficult by the person's lack of ability to understand what has happened to them or around them.

SELF-AWARENESS

The person may be very aware of their disability and how other people view them. They may have difficulty coming to terms with their intellectual disabilities. The person may also be aware of the things that tend to happen at certain times in life. For example people tend to have their first boyfriend or girlfriend in their teenage years, leave the parental home in their twenties or get a full-time job after leaving school or college. People with intellectual disabilities may very well have these goals, but it will probably be more difficult for them to achieve them.

LEARNING EXPERIENCES

The experiences we have in childhood tend to shape our personality in adulthood. People with intellectual disabilities are more likely to have negative learning experiences in childhood, such as failing to keep up with other children at school, failing to do things that their brothers or sisters can do and sometimes not being able to communicate their needs.

Social factors
SOCIAL NETWORKS

People with intellectual disabilities may have limited social networks outside of their home and limited personal resources to increase these networks. This may affect their mental health.

DEMANDS

Sometimes we may place too high or too low demands on people with intellectual disabilities. If demands are too high, we are setting people up to fail; if they are too low, we are decreasing their independence. Both will have an effect on the person's self-esteem.

LACK OF ACTIVITY

Just like anyone else, people with intellectual disabilities need a varied life with different things to do. More often than not they have very little to do, which can have a detrimental effect on their mental health.

Mental health assessment
Mental health problems in people with intellectual disabilities are best assessed by a range of health and social care professionals using a multi-disciplinary approach. These professionals and the services they work in are described in Chapter 3. The aims of the assessment are to:

- Clarify what the problem is

- Find out how the problem is affecting the person's day-to-day life

- Find out what, if anything, is causing or contributing to the mental health problem

Health and social care professionals will achieve these aims through several different methods.

Interviewing the person and their carer

A mental health professional (usually a doctor and/or a nurse) will talk to the person with intellectual disabilities. Where the person you care for has difficulty in communicating, you may be asked the questions. The interview will look at two main areas, the person's current situation and their history.

CURRENT SITUATION

- Why is this person seeing a health/social care professional now?

- What is the person normally like?

- What has changed?

- Are there any possible signs and symptoms of a mental health problem?

- Have there been any recent life events or changes?

  ○ Changes in the family home, changes at the day centre, bereavements and losses etc.

HISTORICAL INFORMATION

- Family history

  ○ People within the family (past and present), mental health problems within the family, how the person gets on with family members

- Personal history
  - When they started to walk, talk etc., schooling, life events, relationships, employment, their abilities and disabilities

- Medical history
  - Past illnesses, the person's ability to report illness, treatments etc.

- Psychiatric history
  - Past illnesses, treatment etc.

- Personality
  - Whether they are sociable or shy, their character, normal mood, their attitudes towards life and other people

Physical examination

There are a number of medical conditions that can make someone look as though they have a mental health problem or that can make the person more likely to have a mental health problem. Also signs and symptoms of some mental health problems can be due to drugs or alcohol. The side effects of some prescribed medications can falsely appear as a mental health problem. These need to be ruled out, so the person can get the right diagnosis and treatment. Additionally, tests may be needed such as:

- Blood test
- X-ray
- Scans
- Urine test

Diagnosis and treatment

After all the information has been gathered the multi-disciplinary team will build a picture of what the problem is and make a diagnosis. From the diagnosis an appropriate management care plan will be written, which is tailored to the needs and wishes of the person involved. Care plans will be holistic, which means that they will look at the person as a whole (e.g. likes and dislikes, activities, short- and long-term goals) and what has made the person vulnerable to a mental health problem. Care plans will involve a wide range of interventions such as taking medication, seeing a counsellor and improving the person's social situation. Therapeutic interventions are described in detail in Chapter 4.

General advice to you as a carer

Preparing information for the assessment

If the person cannot communicate or finds it difficult to tell others his or her thoughts and feelings there are several things that you can do before going to a mental health assessment. This mainly involves having the following information ready:

- An accurate description of what is normal for the person you care for and what has changed

- Information about when these changes started, how often they occur and what impact they have on the person and their life

- Particular changes that the professional will want to know about:

  ○ Sleep pattern (are there any difficulties in sleeping?)
  ○ Appetite and weight
  ○ Are they engaging in their usual routine of activities?
  ○ Are they communicating with others?
  ○ Are they socializing with others?
  ○ Has their behaviour become challenging or more challenging than usual?
  ○ Have they spoken about any strange experiences such as hearing voices when no one is around or strange thoughts or beliefs that are out of character?

Supporting the person with the assessment

Having appointments with doctors and nurses can make anyone anxious. It can be even more anxiety-provoking if you have difficulty in understanding what is going on around you. But there are several things that can be done to reduce the person's anxiety and help them understand what is going on:

- Inform the health or social care professional of any special needs the person you care for may have before the meeting, including communication, visual and physical accessibility needs

- Try to explain to the person beforehand what they will be doing, when it will take place, who will be there and maybe the types of things they might be asked. In some cases this may make him or her more anxious, but you as the person's carer will know best. Ask the person you care for if they would wish to prepare in advance what they want to say to the professional and bring along communication aids etc.

- If the person really does not like going to clinics or hospitals, then ask if you could have a home visit

- If the person you care for is easily distracted or has a lot to say, you may want to book a longer appointment or have the assessment over two or three appointments

- There are some useful books that you can use to help prepare the person for the assessment. You could see if your social worker or nurse could get hold of them for you: they are called 'Books Beyond Words' and they are published by Gaskell Press

- If the meeting is going to be held somewhere the person you care for has never been before perhaps they could visit beforehand, so they can get used to the place

- Sometimes (though it is getting a lot better) professionals ask questions to the carer and not the person themselves. You should do your best to help the person communicate their thoughts and feelings to the professional

General steps you can take to help the person

The list below is general and applies to all mental health problems. In Chapter 2 at the end of each section you will find additional information about what to do and how to help the person with reference to specific mental health problems.

DURING THE ASSESSMENT PERIOD

- Encourage the person to ask questions about the mental health problem and possible treatment or ask on their behalf especially if he or she is not able to ask questions for him or herself, or to concentrate on the information given

- Encourage the person to take part in decisions about their treatment as much as possible

- A trusting and co-operative relationship between individuals, carers, and health professionals will help to manage the mental health problem better. All mental health professionals know that working with the family or other carers is essential and that families are usually an important part of the treatment team, implementing at home the strategies decided together at the clinic

- Plan in advance and be prepared. With the help of a mental health professional agree what steps to take or whom to contact (have a list of phone numbers) if there is a problem. This will make the whole experience less stressful for both you and the person you care for

- Ask for more information and advice. Self-help groups, leaflets and books may be helpful in explaining the diagnosis clearly. Also carers' organizations and self-help groups are a good source of specialized information and contact. These are listed throughout this Guide along with their contact details

- You may need to ask the doctor about the medication being prescribed:

    ○ What is the medication?

- What is the dose?
- How does it work?
- What are the unwanted side effects to expect?
- Is psychotherapy treatment available? (see description in Chapter 4)

AFTERWARDS: LIVING WITH THE MENTAL HEALTH PROBLEM

Learning to cope with ongoing mental health problems can be hard work. But there are a few things you can do to make the experience easier for you and the person you care for:

- You can help to remind the person to attend their appointments with doctors and mental health professionals, and to stay in touch with services

- It is also important to ensure that the person you care for gets medical advice before stopping treatment. If treatments including medication are stopped too soon symptoms may return

- Discourage less helpful ways of trying to cope such as drinking alcohol

- Encourage the person to keep doing their daily activities

- Work with the person and the mental health professionals towards identifying the early warning signs of the problem. Early detection of these signs can help to prevent the person from relapsing and symptoms deteriorating further; the relapse might be less severe. There are great advantages of keeping alert to early warning signs. This is particularly important if the person you care for chooses not to accept or continue long-term medications but instead relies on early intervention and help following the detection of early warning signs

Some individuals experiencing a relapse will very quickly lose their usual judgement and insight and fail to view changes in their mood and behaviour as being a problem. Your involvement is especially important for monitoring the characteristic pattern of warning signs and symptoms that may indicate that the person is becoming ill again:

- You will need to be alert to these changes and be prepared to take appropriate action.

- Use your contact list and contact the appropriate health professionals early

- Early intervention usually includes things like medication review and increased contact and support from the mental health professionals as well as quick access to services when required

- Ask the person what steps they would like you to take and how they would like to be treated if they become ill again (by thinking back to the last time they were ill). Also, help the person to keep a list of things that might help them to reduce stress as this increases the possibility of becoming ill again. For example, pleasant activities such as listening to music or visiting a good friend can help the person and avoid worsening of the symptoms

After a long period of being ill or hospitalized the person you care for might have lost their skills, motivation and self-esteem. They might need you to help them with things they could previously do by themselves. The impact of the caring role might be overwhelming for you. Getting practical help, emotional support and respite can help to ease some of the problems you might face.

Your relationship with the person you care for can be particularly important at this point as it provides them with all kinds of support and can remind them of their life and identity before becoming unwell. It can also remind them that life can go on in much the same way as before. It can also be an extra challenging time for you as a carer.

How to deal with difficult behaviours[2]

Sleeping or withdrawing a lot of the time, or sleeping at odd times

- Leave the person alone but make some contact whenever he or she comes out of their room to let them know you are there if they need you

- Gently encourage passive activities that are not too demanding (e.g. watching TV, going for a short walk)

- Occasionally offer a cup of tea or coffee

- Slowly ask the person to get up earlier in the day and to do more things. Offer something to enjoy when he or she gets up, like a tempting breakfast or pleasant music

- Praise him or her for getting up

If the person has been well for some time and develops sleeping difficulties or begins to withdraw again, contact his or her clinician. This behaviour could be a sign of relapsing.

Inactivity and not feeling like doing anything

- Leave the person alone if he or she does not want to do anything

- If the person says they are bored, offer or suggest some simple activity such as listening to music or watching a video

- Try different activities to find out what the person will enjoy

- Try to have a regular daily routine so that things are predictable and encourage him or her to join in or follow this daily routine

- When the person starts getting better, give him or her simple daily chores to do. Break chores into small steps if they are difficult

- Try to make allowances for the person if he or she needs to do things like eating at unusual times

- Offer rewards and praise for the times when the person does the chores, even if the chores are not done perfectly

- Get advice from the person's clinician about when he is ready to do various things and how to encourage him to do these things

- Try not to nag or criticize the person and don't label the person as 'lazy' – this label doesn't help either of you

- Try not to wear yourself out doing everything for the person

Aggressive behaviour

People with schizophrenia are usually shy and withdrawn. Aggression is no more common among these people than in the general community. However, if you're living with someone who does tend to be aggressive, you will need to know what to do when he or she becomes aggressive so that you feel more able to cope in these situations:

- Give a firm command such as 'stop please'. If the person doesn't stop, leave the room or the house quickly

- Leave the person alone until they have calmed down. If you've left the house, a phone call may tell you if he or she is calmer

- Call the person's clinician, or the Crisis Team if one is available in your area. Your local hospital or community mental health centre will inform you

- Take any threats or warnings seriously and contact the clinician or doctor, particularly if the person has ideas of being persecuted

- Afterwards you can say, 'I know you were upset but we won't put up with violence, ever', or 'You can tell us what you're angry about, but you cannot hit anybody'

- If you're afraid for your safety over a period of time you may need to arrange to have someone else stay with you or be available on the phone, or to arrange for the person to stay elsewhere

- Discuss any threats and violence openly in the family and with the clinician
- Try to see what triggers the aggression and stop or avoid that situation (e.g. overcrowding in the house, criticism)
- If all else fails, it's OK to call the police if you or your family need protection
- Try not to argue or say angry, critical things that will provoke more aggression
- Don't stay around if the person doesn't calm down and don't tolerate aggression or violence to you or your family
- Don't let yourself or the family become the only ones the person depends on as this can create anger

Not taking prescribed medication

- If the problem is a result of forgetting, gently remind the person when it is time to take the medicine
- Find a daily routine (e.g. breakfast) when taking medication can become a habit
- Remind the person calmly that medication helps to keep them well
- Ask if the person has any side effects
- Talk to the doctor about the person's difficulty with remembering to take medication
- If he or she refuses to take medication, let the doctor know if symptoms get worse or reappear

Health screening

As people with intellectual disabilities often do not report illnesses, it can be useful for you to arrange regular health screening with the person's GP or practice nurse. This will help identify treatable problems with vision or hearing, obesity, skin infections, diabetes and other conditions. Also, it is important for you to review care at times of transition (e.g. leaving school). Encourage the person to see the same doctor or nurse at each appointment, if possible, to build trust and reduce problems in communication.

Regular check-ups can be organized with local general medical practitioners, dentists and other relevant health professionals. The individual may find it helpful to use a calendar and fill in a reminder showing when the next check-up is due. You can help the person by reminding them and by helping them to make and keep appointments. Ideally the person you care for will be the one who takes responsibility for his or her own physical health. The following check-ups may be particularly important:

- Dental care for tooth decay, gum disease or other dental problems
- Podiatry for injured or painful feet
- Pelvic examinations (pap smears) to detect early cervical changes or sexually transmitted diseases
- Breast screening
- Prostate and testicular checks
- Blood tests to detect anaemia and monitor the effects of or levels of certain medicines (e.g. those given for some kinds of epilepsy, thyroid disorders)
- Screening for skin cancers
- Diabetes
- Diet and nutrition
- Optometry

Notes

1   'Learning disabilities' is the term used in the UK for 'intellectual disabilities.'
2   Also see Andrews, G. and Jenkins, R. (eds) (1999) *Management of Mental Disorders (UK Edition)*. Sydney: World Health Organisation Collaborating Centre for Mental Health and Substance Abuse.

Resources

African-Caribbean Mental Health Service
Zion Community Health and Resource Centre
Royce Road
Hulme
Manchester M15 5FQ
Tel: 0161 226 9562
Fax: 0161 227 9862

(Counselling, support, self-advocacy, drop-in facilities)

Carers Association of Ireland
St Mary's Community Centre
Richmond Hill
Dublin 6
Ireland
Tel: +353 (0) 1 497 4498
Website: www.carersireland.com

Carers Line
Tel: 0808 808 7777 (Mon–Fri 10am–12pm and 2pm–4pm)

(A helpline for carers to discuss any issue)

Carers National Association
20–25 Glasshouse Yard
London EC1A 4JT
Tel: 020 8808 7777
Email: info@ukcarers.org

(Campaigns for carers' rights and helpline)

Chinese Mental Health Association
Oxford House
Derbyshire Street
London E2 6HG
Tel: 020 7613 1008
Fax: 020 7613 1008
Email: admin@cmha.demon.co.uk

(Advocacy, befriending, interpretation, holistic therapy, counselling, mental health promotion and housing advice)

Department of Health – Learning Disabilities
Website: www.dh.gov.uk/policyandguidance/healthandsocialcaretopics/learningdisabilities/fs/en

(Information on current government policy)

Department of Health – Mental Health

Website: www.dh.gov.uk/policyandguidance/healthandsocialcaretopics/
mentalhealth/fs/en

(Information on current government policy)

Edinburgh Association for Mental Health

40 Shandwick Place
Edinburgh EH2 4RT
Tel: 0131 225 8508
Fax: 0131 220 0028
Website: www.oneworld.org/eamh
Email: eamh@freeuk.com

(Information/resource centre, befriending, counselling, advocacy)

Estia

Estia Centre
Munro – Guy's Hospital
66 Snowsfields
London SE1 3SS
Tel: 020 7378 3218
Website: www.estiacentre.org

(Provides training, research and development for those who support adults with learning disabilities and additional mental health and/or challenging needs)

Foundation for People with Learning Disabilities

83 Victoria Street
London SW1H 0HW
Tel: 020 7802 0300
Fax: 020 7802 0301
Website: www.fpld.org.uk
Email: fpld@fpld.org.uk

(A series of published booklets on different mental health problems such as anxiety, depression, dementia, bulimia, and other issues concerning positive mental health for children and adults with learning disabilities)

Gaskell Publications

(A series of books called 'Books Beyond Words' which may help you to explain certain issues to the person with intellectual disabilities. For information see www.rcpsych.ac.uk/publications/bbw/) See Royal College of Psychiatrists for further contact details.

Institute for Complementary Medicine
PO BOX 194
London SE16 7QZ
Tel: 020 7237 5765
Website: www.icmedicine.co.uk
Email: icm@icmmedicine.co.uk

(Information about natural therapies)

Jewish Association for the Mentally Ill (JAMI)
16a North End Road
London NW11 7PH
Tel: 020 8458 2223
Fax: 020 8458 1117
Website: www.mentalhealth-jami.org.uk
Email: ruthjami@hotmail.com

(Support for younger members of the community, families and carers)

LBHF (Leeds Black Health Forum)
The Resource Centre
Bushbury House
4 Laurel Mount
St Mary's Road
Leeds LS7 3JX
Tel: 0113 237 4229
Fax: 0113 237 4230

(Support, advocacy and counselling for people from Africa, Asia and the Caribbean)

Manaseek
18 Elm Grove
Eccleston Park
Prescot
Liverpool L34 2RX
Tel: 0151 426 0336/01704 506056
Helpline: 0151 426 3121
Email: rajpal@arya6.freeserve.co.uk

(24-hour helpline for anyone. Special group: Asian men and women)

Mental Health Foundation
Website: www.mentalhealth.org.uk
Email: mhf@mhf.org.uk
(Information on mental health problems, services and where to get help)

England
Seventh Floor
83 Victoria Street
London SW1 0HW
Tel: 020 7802 0300

Scotland
Fifth Floor
Merchants House
30 George Square
Glasgow G2 1EG
Tel: 0141 572 0125
Email: Scotland@mhf.org.uk

The Mental Health Shop

40 Chandos Street
Leicester LE2 1BL
Tel: 0116 247 1525
Fax: 0116 255 3625
Website: www.mentalhealthshop.org.uk
Email: bmhgrc.mhs@care4free.net

(Information, advice and support for African, Caribbean and Asian people)

MIND (National Association for Mental Health)

15–19 Broadway
London E15 4BQ
Tel: 020 8519 2122
MindinfoLine: 0845 766 0163 (Mon–Fri 9.15am–4.45pm)
Website: www.mind.org.uk
Email: contact@mind.org.uk

MIND has many branches across the UK. Please call the info line or visit the website for your local branch.

(Information and fact sheets)

MIND Cymru (Wales)

Third Floor
Quebec House
Castlebridge
5–19 Cowbridge Road East
Cardiff CF11 9AB
Tel: 029 2039 5123

National Association for the Dually Diagnosed (NADD)

132 Fair Street
Kingston
New York 12401
Tel: (800) 331 5362 or (845) 331-4336
Fax: (845) 331 4569
Website: www.thenadd.org
Email: info@thenadd.org

(An association established for professionals, care providers and families to promote understanding of and services for individuals who have developmental disabilities and mental health needs)

NHS Direct, England and Wales

Tel: 0845 46 47

(24-hour helpline on any health issue)

NHS Helpline for Scotland

Tel: 0800 22 44 88

Northern Ireland Association for Mental Health

Beacon House
80 University Street
Belfast BT7 1HE
Tel: 028 9032 8474
Fax: 028 9023 4940
Website: www.niamh.co.uk

(Residential, day care and counselling information, leaflets and booklets)

Royal College of Psychiatrists

17 Belgrave Square
London SW1X 8PG
Tel: 020 7235 2351
Website: www.rcpsych.ac.uk
Email: rcpsych@rcpsych.ac.uk

(Information and fact sheets)

Sainsbury Centre for Mental Health

134 Borough High Street
London
SE1 1LB
Tel: 020 7827 8300
Website: www.scmh.org.uk
Email: contact@scmh.org.uk

(Information on current issues and services)

SANE

First Floor
Cityside House
40 Adler Street
London E1 1EE
Tel: 020 7375 1002
Fax: 020 7375 2162
Helpline: 0845 767 8000 (12pm–2am every day of the year)
Website: www.sane.org.uk
Email: info@sane.org.uk

(Information and fact sheets on mental health problems and treatments, support for carers)

The Tamarind Centre

(Coventry Black Mental Health)
Harp Place
2 Sandy Lane
Radford
Coventry CV1 4DX
Tel: 02476 227 712
Fax: 02476 6333 772
Helpline: 02476 225 512

(Support to Asian, African and African-Caribbean people, advocacy, counselling, drop-in sessions, outreach, befriending and information)

Vishvas Project

Confederation of Indian Organisations (UK)
5 Westminster Bridge Road
London SE1 7XW
Tel: 020 7928 9889
Helpline: 020 7620 4025
Email: ciovishvas@aol.com

(Mental health service for the South Asian Community. Counselling, befriending and support for South Asian women in Southwark and Lambeth)

YoungMinds

102–108 Clerkenwell Road
London EC1M 5SA
Tel: 020 7336 8445
Fax: 020 7336 8446
Website: www.youngminds.org.uk
Email: enquiries@youngminds.org.uk

(Parents' information service, leaflets and booklets, children and young people)

Chapter 2

Mental Health Problems

Geraldine Holt, Anastasia Gratsa and Steve Hardy

Affective disorders
Schizophrenia
Anxiety disorders
Adjustment disorders and acute stress disorder
Dementia
Eating disorders
Substance misuse
Personality disorders

Affective disorders

Affective disorders are mental health problems that are characterized by abnormal changes in the person's mood. They include depression, mania and bipolar affective disorder (formally known as manic depression).

> Paul is 22 and has severe intellectual disabilities. He lives with three other men with intellectual disabilities in a house that has 24-hour staffing. Paul enjoys a wide range of activities at home and in the community. He cannot talk but shows people his needs by leading them to what he wants. The staff are becoming concerned about him. Recently he has been refusing to go to his morning activities and is generally not eating breakfast or lunch, normally his favourite meals. He has also lost weight. Paul has also started to bang his head against the wall or floor when staff

ask him to help around the house. This is something he has never done before. The night staff have also reported that he is getting up in the night and finding it difficult to sleep.

Depression

Depression is one of our most common emotions. It is common to experience feelings of sadness and tiredness in response to life events such as losses or disappointments. In most cases, as people come to terms with changes in life, the sad feelings resolve. In situations such as bereavement, these feelings may continue for months and return at significant times such as birthdays or anniversaries of the lost friend or family member who has died. Sometimes people continue to feel sad for longer periods and develop feelings that interfere with their ability to cope with everyday life. This is the type of depression that needs specialist help. People who are depressed may experience some of the following:

- Persistent feeling of low mood
- Loss of interest in usual activities
- Loss of energy
- Changes in sleep pattern
- Changes in appetite and weight
- Not socializing as much as normal
- Low self-esteem and a lack of confidence
- Not wanting to communicate with others
- Feeling guilty or blaming yourself about things that you normally would not
- Feelings of wanting to hurt yourself or end your life
- Not being able to concentrate
- Feeling irritable and losing your patience with other people

In severe depression people may experience psychotic symptoms, and the context of these tends to be in line with the person's low mood. They may have hallucinations, such as hearing voices telling them they are worthless or bad. Sometimes people have delusions, for example someone might think they are rotting away inside or they are to blame for something bad that has happened in the world (e.g. a disaster).

In people with severe intellectual disabilities depression may present as a new or an increase in challenging behaviour. Such behaviour may include self-injury, aggression and screaming. You might also notice that the person cannot or is unwilling to do things for themselves like they used to. Those who are normally continent might have incidents of incontinence.

One of the main problems in diagnosing depression in people with severe or profound intellectual disabilities is their limited verbal and non-verbal communication and difficulty in expressing how they feel. Carers have an important role in helping the mental health professional to make the diagnosis. Because you know the person, their likes and dislikes, you can notice changes in mood, sleep, energy, appetite etc.

Some people may have one episode of depression in their lifetime, whereas others may have re-occurring episodes. Depression is very common. In fact one out of four people in the wider community are likely to visit their GP at some time in their life because they feel depressed.

How can you help the person you care for?

A person with depression is not lazy or weak because they find it 'difficult to get out of bed' or because they do not find anything 'worthwhile or pleasurable'. They cannot just 'snap out of it', 'pull themselves together' or 'get better with a good holiday'. They often feel guilty and blame themselves because they are doing less, thus adding to the feelings of depression.

Depression affects the person's thoughts, feelings and everyday functioning. Friends, family and carers can support the person to overcome depression by keeping busy, avoiding negative thinking, solving problems, and reducing stress:

- Encourage and support the individual to start the day with an activity that gives him or her pleasure and a positive sense of achievement

- Encourage and support the person to plan pleasant activities in advance. This will give him or her a sense of control over their lives and a structure so that on the day nothing seems so overwhelming

- Encourage the person to take up exercise. Exercise can increase the body's metabolism and counteract the chemical imbalance associated with depression. It can also provide a distraction from negative thoughts and give a sense of control by engaging in a self-disciplined activity that promotes well-being

Be aware that life events, medical problems and a stressful home environment make an individual more vulnerable to further incidents of depression:

- Depression can be a serious mental health problem. It is important to remember that people with depression sometimes have thoughts of harming themselves. If you have concern about any risks of self-harm try and talk to the person and his/her doctor about it. Listen to the person's feelings of depression but also point out that help is available

- Try to distract the person by involving him or her in pleasant, low-key activities with someone he or she knows well

- Let the person know that you accept and care about him or her

- Consider whether any stressful things can be removed which might be depressing for the person (e.g. too much pressure at work)

- Do not insist on the person doing much or going out and try not to nag or criticize them

- Do not wear yourself out by doing everything for them

Sometimes if a person is having difficulties with sleeping, cutting out coffee and cola can help.

Most episodes of depression improve after a few months. Although depression can be treated effectively, it can come back. Be aware of the warning signs and seek advice as soon as possible. Early intervention can help to avoid further deterioration and aid quick recovery (see also Chapter 4).

Bipolar affective disorder or manic depression

The term **bipolar affective disorder** is used for people who experience depressive, manic or mixed episodes (characteristics of depression and mania together) at different times. People usually recover and have a period of stability between episodes. Depressive episodes are far more common and tend to last longer. Manic episodes tend to start quite quickly and are generally shorter. It is very rare for people just to have manic episodes, without an earlier or later depressive episode.

> John has moderate intellectual disabilities. He lives in a supported house and attends a day centre. Over the past few weeks he has not been sleeping well. He has been restless, not even sitting to eat, but instead grabbing the food in his hands and wolfing it down. He has been irritable and argumentative, and has attempted to take over some of the personal care tasks of the staff with other clients. When asked not to do this he becomes both physically and verbally aggressive, saying he can do the job better than them.

Mania

Mania is an emotional state of intense energy and hyperactivity with no apparent reason. People who have mania will experience some of the following:

- Feeling elated and euphoric
- Sudden changes in mood, such as being irritable and quarrelsome
- Great difficulty in sleeping
- Being overactive and excessively energetic
- Changes in appetite and generally loss of weight
- Talking too much and very fast
- Behaving impulsively

- Interfering with those around them
- Being very demanding
- Doing things they would never dream of doing when they were well, because of embarrassment
- Losing their inhibitions both socially and sexually
- Not being able to concentrate and being easily distracted

In severe mania people may also experience psychotic symptoms. The content of these tend to be in agreement with the person's elated mood. For example they may have hallucinations, such as hearing voices telling them how wonderful they are and that they can do anything. Sometimes people have delusions, such as believing they are related to the royal family or that they have super powers.

Mania can lead to severe consequences for the person, such as:

- Exhaustion
- Dehydration
- Weight loss
- Unplanned pregnancies and/or sexually transmitted diseases
- Financial problems

How can you help the person you care for?
DURING DEPRESSED MOODS

Please refer to the advice for depression which is given earlier in this chapter.

DURING MANIC PERIODS

Avoid argument and confrontation unless necessary to prevent harmful acts. The person you care for may be convinced that he or she is right, although to you and others their thoughts are irrational. Also take care regarding impulsive or dangerous behaviour. Sometimes close observation by family members or others is needed to prevent the person getting into trouble (e.g. debt because they overspend their money, trouble with the police for inappropriate behaviour in public).

If you or the person is able to identify early symptoms of forthcoming 'highs' then advise and encourage them to:

- Stop consumption of tea and coffee and other caffeine-based food and drink that act as stimulants

- Avoid stimulating or stressful situations

- Plan for a good night's sleep

- Take relaxing exercise during the day (e.g. swimming or a walk before bed)

- Take steps to limit their ability to spend money

Resources

Aware (for Ireland and Northern Ireland)
72 Lower Leeson Street
Dublin 2
Republic of Ireland
Tel: +353 (0) 1 676 6166
Website: www.aware.ie

CRUSE Bereavement Care
Cruse House
126 Sheen Road
Richmond
Surrey TW9 1UR
Helpline: 020 8940 4818 (Mon–Fri 9.30am–5pm)
Website: www.crusebereavementcare.org.uk

(Information and advice on bereavement and dealing with a major personal crisis)

Depression Alliance
Website: www.depressionalliance.org
Email: information@depressionalliance.org

(Information on depression, treatment and associated issues)

England
35 Westminster Bridge Road
London SE1 7JB
Tel: 020 7633 0557

Scotland
3 Grosvenor Gardens
Edinburgh EH12 5JU
Tel: 0131 467 3050

Cymru (Wales)
11 Plas Melin
Westbourne Road
Whitchurch
Cardiff CF4 2BT
Tel: 029 2069 2891

Manic Depression Fellowship
Website: www.mdf.org.uk
Email: mdf@mdf.org.uk

(Information on manic depression, treatment and associated issues)

England
Castleworks
21 St Georges Street
London SE1 6ES
Tel: 020 7793 2600

Scotland
Studio 1019
Mile End Mill
Abbey Mill Business Park
Paisley PA1 1PG
Tel: 0141 560 2050
Website: www.rcvsweb.co.uk/mdf/index.php

Wales
1 Palmyra Place
Newport
Gwent NP20 4EJ
Tel: 01633 244244
Helpline: 08456 340 080
Email: info@mdf.org.uk

Samaritans
Tel: 0345 909090
Website: www.samaritans.org

(Support for those feeling lonely, despairing or suicidal)

Schizophrenia

Schizophrenia is a mental illness, which is characterized by profound distortions in the person's thoughts, feelings and behaviour. The person starts to see the world very differently from the way they normally do and from the way others see it. The person loses touch with reality.

Schizophrenia can happen to anyone but is more likely to affect people for the first time in their early twenties. Some people will only have one episode of schizophrenia and will make a full recovery; unfortunately others do not and will have further episodes.

There are a number of core signs and symptoms of schizophrenia, which are described below. However, each person who has schizophrenia is likely to be affected very differently from another.

Hallucinations

Auditory hallucinations are common in schizophrenia. Voices may give a running commentary on what the person is doing, make insulting remarks or may tell the person to do something. The voices tend to say negative things and they are usually very distressing for the person.

Delusions

Delusions are false beliefs. In schizophrenia delusions can have many themes, but one of the most common is persecutory beliefs. For example the person may believe that everybody hates them or keeps staring at them. Another common theme is that others or machines can read their mind or have the power to take their thoughts away or place new thoughts into their mind.

Thought disorder

This is where the person has problems in organizing their thoughts and results in others having great difficulty in understanding them due to their speech being disorganized. When the person talks everything can sound jumbled up and sometimes they will make up words that do not exist, for example 'I never eat sphericks'.

It may be difficult to recognize these symptoms in a person with intellectual disabilities if they are unable to describe them. However, the person's behaviour may suggest their presence, e.g. if they keep brushing at their clothes as if to remove something, or start to shout or talk to someone that no one else is aware of. Sometimes people with intellectual disabilities show these behaviours ordinarily, e.g. talking to themselves. *It is when there is a change that we are alerted to the possibility of there being a health problem.*

The symptoms described above are psychotic symptoms. These happen when the person is at their most unwell and they are usually treated with medication immediately. But there is another side to schizophrenia that can happen when the psychotic symptoms have decreased. The person can have a loss of motivation and energy levels. They may find it difficult to do everyday tasks. It is important that this is seen as part of the mental health problem and the person is not just seen as lazy.

> Jane is 22 years old and lives with her parents. She has mild intellectual disabilities and has an active social life and has a boyfriend. She goes to a day centre four days a week. Jane's key worker has informed her mother that her behaviour has been a bit odd at the centre lately. She isn't socializing with her friends like she normally does and spends long periods of time alone with her hands over her ears. Staff have also noticed that she appears to be talking to herself quite a lot. Jane's mum says she's been a bit strange at home as well. She will now only eat food that comes straight out of a wrapper. Jane will not touch anything cooked by her mum; she says that it has been poisoned.

How can you help the person you care for?

If the person you care for sees or hears things that you do not see or hear, or speaks to himself or to 'voices':

- Keep calm

- Try to distract the person if you can by: involving the person in something interesting; offering something to look at (e.g. magazine); asking the person to help you find something (e.g. to find the newspaper); engaging the person in pleasant conversation; encouraging the person to be with other people he or she knows well

- Encourage him or her to use their coping mechanisms (e.g. relax, avoid crowded places or listen to a personal stereo in order to distract themselves)

- Don't panic or assume that another breakdown is occurring and don't act horrified

- Don't try and figure out what he or she is talking about or to whom

- Don't let others laugh about these hallucinations or strange talk

- Don't ask the person to try to *force* the voices to stop

Strange talk or beliefs:

- Don't allow the family to make jokes or criticize the person

- Don't argue about the strange ideas – arguing never changes the ideas and only upsets both of you

- Don't spend much time listening and don't pretend you understand talk that makes no sense to you. It's better to say clearly that you don't like the strange talk

- Don't keep looking at the person or nodding your head if they are speaking strangely

- Don't keep up a conversation that you feel is distressing, or annoying, or too confusing for you. It's OK to say, 'I'll talk to you later when you're making more sense'

- Don't look horrified or embarrassed by strange talk

We know that people with mental health problems and often their families are stigmatized, misunderstood and rejected by society's ignorance of mental health problems. Stigma is a sense of shame projected by society to the person that is to be blamed and avoided. This is very hurtful to the person who experiences mental health problems and also their family. Meeting people from families who have similar problems helps to reduce the stigma and isolation associated with having a family member who suffers from schizophrenia. Carers' organizations and self-help groups (such as Hearing Voices Network) are a good source of specialized information, advice and contact (see Resources section below).

Resources

Hearing Voices Network

91 Oldham Street
Manchester M4 1LW
Tel: 0161 834 5768
Helpline: 0161 834 5768
Website: www.hearing-voices.org
Email: hearingvoices@care4free.net

(Support network for people who hear voices and for relatives, carers and workers. Self-help groups throughout the UK.)

Making Space

18b Otley Road
Headingley
Leeds LS6 2AD
Tel: 0113 274 6010
Fax: 0113 274 5528

46 Allen Street
Warrington WA2 7JB
Tel: 01925 571680
Fax: 01925 231402

(Local support and advice to people who have schizophrenia and their families in the North of England)

National Schizophrenia Fellowship of Scotland

Claremont House
130 East Claremont Street
Edinburgh EH7 4LB
Tel: 0131 557 8969
Website: www.nsfscot.org.uk
Email: info@nsfscot.org.uk

(Information on schizophrenia and associated issues)

Rethink

(Previously called National Schizophrenia Fellowship)
30 Tabernacle Street
London EC2A 4DD
Advice Line: 020 8974 6814 (Mon–Fri 10am–3pm)
Website: www.rethink.org
Email: info@rethink.org

(Information on schizophrenia and associated issues)

Anxiety disorders

Anxiety is a physical and psychological reaction to something that is seen as threatening. Anxiety is a normal human reaction that in some cases can be beneficial. For example, when going to a job interview, feelings of anxiety can make a person more alert. However, when the feelings of anxiety continue and are out of proportion with the actual danger of the situation and affect the person's day-to-day life it becomes a mental health problem.

> Clara is 35 years old and has moderate intellectual disabilities. Clara and her parents have recently moved to a new town. Shortly after moving Clara's mum noticed that she was reluctant to leave the house. She put this down to her settling in. To cheer Clara up she took her to the local shopping centre to buy some new clothes. During the car journey Clara was unusually quiet. Once in the car park she became very clingy, refusing to let go of her mum's hand. As they walked through the centre entrance, Clara started to breathe very quickly. She was hot and sweaty and started to scream. Her mum took her home immediately. Now every time her mum suggests even leaving the house Clara starts to shake and runs to her bedroom. Clara is now refusing to leave the house at all.

There are several different types of anxiety disorder, but most have similar signs and symptoms, which are described below:

- Breathing becomes faster
- Heart beats faster
- Sweaty and clammy skin
- Dry mouth
- Muscular tension
- Upset stomach
- Sleep disturbance
- Heightened senses and alertness

People with intellectual disabilities may also show the following behaviours when they are anxious:

- They may become clingy to those they feel safe with

- They may need extra reassurance

- They may self-injure or become aggressive when they are in situations they find threatening

The different types of anxiety disorders

PHOBIA

A phobia is an irrational fear of the danger posed by an object or situation. The person will avoid the object or the situation. Phobias can be restrictive and disrupt a person's life. The person might be afraid of open spaces (agoraphobia), heights, animals or injections, for instance.

Social phobia is a constant, irrational fear linked to the presence of other people and the fear of acting in an embarrassing way. Activities carried out in the presence of others (e.g. eating in a restaurant or using public toilets) might cause extreme anxiety.

Some people with intellectual disabilities may have had restricted lives with limited opportunities to try something new. If they are presented with a new activity this might cause them anxiety, which may be misinterpreted as a phobia.

PANIC DISORDER

A panic attack is an experience of intense fear accompanied by breathlessness, dizziness, palpitations, and often nausea and chest pain. Most people know that this is a passing situation but some people think these features are warning signs of a heart attack, faint or loss of control. Such frightening thoughts can lead to even more fear, which in turn can cause more intense bodily symptoms, creating a vicious circle. The more the person concentrates on these bodily sensations the more frightened he or she will feel. Some people with panic disorder also have agoraphobia (a fear of open spaces).

OBSESSIVE COMPULSIVE DISORDER

Obsessions are thoughts, images or impulses that come to mind. They may appear irrational and uncontrollable to the person experiencing them.

Everyone experiences obsessions from time to time but sometimes they interfere with everyday life.

A compulsion is a repetitive act that the person feels they must perform. A person with intellectual disabilities may not be able to describe their thoughts about their repetitive act. The activity is clearly excessive and sometimes it takes the form of a ritual. Compulsions are often to do with cleanliness, the fear of contamination or tidiness and precision. Sometimes they take up most of the day and interfere with the person's social or everyday life. This is usually by wasting time with repetitive, magical, protective practices such as counting, saying particular numbers and checking things (gas, light switches, locks, windows and doors etc.). Interfering with the person's compulsions can cause him or her distress and aggression. This can be extremely distressing and tiring for the person and the carer. Compulsions are commonly seen in people with autism.

POST-TRAUMATIC STRESS DISORDER

Traumatic or life threatening events (e.g. sexual or physical assault or mugging, severe car accident) have psychological effects. For the majority of people these decrease very soon after the event. Some, however, continue to experience symptoms of irritability, memory and/or concentration problems, low mood, loss of interest, problems at work and physical problems. Also, the person might experience unpleasant memories, nightmares and flashbacks. The person may try to avoid thoughts, activities and situations that will remind him or her of what happened.

GENERALIZED ANXIETY DISORDER

This is sometimes referred to as free-floating anxiety, as it does not occur when the person is confronted with particular situations or threats. Someone with generalized anxiety disorder experiences long-lasting, uncontrollable worry and feelings of apprehension. Complaints such as pounding heart, nausea, chest pain, discomfort, restlessness, lump in the throat, insomnia due to worry, anxiety or fear, difficulty in concentrating, and being easily distracted are common. Symptoms may last for months and occur regularly.

How can you help the person you care for?
ANXIETY

- Remind the person to relax or occupy him or herself with a pre-agreed activity that helps them to unwind

- Encourage the person to use relaxation methods daily to reduce tension (e.g. relaxation or yoga classes). Regular physical exercise is often helpful

- Advise the person you care for to avoid caffeine consumption and the use of alcohol or cigarettes to cope with anxiety

- Encourage the person to engage in pleasurable activities and to resume activities that have been helpful in the past

- Help the person to identify exaggerated worries or pessimistic thoughts and discuss ways to question these worries when they occur

PANIC DISORDER

Panic is common and can be treated. You can support the person to take the right steps in case of an impending attack:

- Advise him or her to stay where they are until the panic passes. This might take up to an hour

- Slow, but not too deep, breathing can help to reduce the physical sensations

- Focus their thinking on something visible (e.g. look at a magazine)

- If hyperventilation occurs, sitting down and breathing into a paper bag can help (this is not advisable if the person suffers from asthma or heart problems)

Support the person to reduce caffeine consumption and avoid alcohol and nicotine to reduce anxiety

OBSESSIVE COMPULSIVE DISORDER

Obsessive compulsive disorder can be a serious mental health problem and treatment interventions are based on behavioural techniques (see Chapter 4 on therapeutic interventions). The person is encouraged to systematically expose themselves to the specific fears underlying the obsessions while also being encouraged not to respond to the obsessions with compulsive behaviours. For example someone who washes their hands repeatedly in fear of contaminating or poisoning themselves will be encouraged to take small steps of what is called 'graded exposure' from a mildly anxious action (e.g. taking the rubbish out without washing hands) to the most stressful action (e.g. handling money and not washing hands afterwards). In taking the rubbish out without washing hands the person will be encouraged not to respond to the obsessive thought ('I feel dirty') with the compulsion ('I need to wash my hands'). Initially the treatment goal is not to cure the problem but for the individual to gain control over these thoughts. The mental health professional will educate the person about the nature of obsessive compulsive disorder, the reasons for exposure and the prevention of responding to the obsessive thoughts.

Most of these rituals (washing hands repeatedly, or checking the gas) take place at home. You can support the person with all of these by:

- Helping the person to maintain new behaviours

- Encouraging the person to practise these new behaviours regularly

- Supporting the person to keep to the ground rules that they have developed as part of the therapeutic intervention (e.g. wash hands once, very quickly, after going to the toilet)

- Avoiding giving reassurance about the possibility of danger (e.g. avoid saying to the person 'you know it is very unlikely that you will poison yourself by not washing your hands'). The person has to learn to confront his or her fears and live with the doubt. These fears should subside eventually

PHOBIAS

Similar principles of 'graded exposure' apply. See section above on obsessive compulsive disorder for advice on what you can do to help the person you care for. Also, depending on the individual situation, encourage the person to use relaxation techniques, breathing exercises or other coping strategies that they have been taught as part of therapeutic interventions.

POST-TRAUMATIC STRESS DISORDER

Suffering from post-traumatic stress disorder is not a weakness. The person needs support and understanding and not to be told 'to snap out of it'.

Avoiding discussion about the traumatic event is unhelpful. Encourage the person to talk about it. Avoiding situations that might trigger memories of the trauma helps to maintain the fears and distress. With professional help, support and encourage the person to face these situations gradually. If severe depression is present be aware of the risk of self-harm and inform the person's doctor. Also, discourage the person from using alcohol or cigarettes to cope with anxiety.

Resources

First Steps to Freedom (Organisation on Obsessive Compulsive Disorder)
7 Avon Court
Kenilworth
Warwickshire CV8 2GX
Helpline: 01926 851608
Website: www.first-steps.org
Email: info@first-steps.org

(General information on obsessive compulsive disorder and other anxiety disorders, self-help groups, leaflets, relaxation tapes)

National Phobics Society
Zion Community Resource Centre
339 Stretford Road
Hulme
Manchester M15 4ZY
Tel: 0870 7700 456
Website: www.phobics-society.org.uk
Email: natphob.soc@good.co.uk

(Information on phobias, treatments and associated issues, local groups, helpline)

No Panic
93 Brands Farm Way
Telford
Shropshire
England TF3 2JQ
Helpline: 0808 808 0545 (10am–10pm every day)
Website: www.nopanic.org.uk
Email: ceo@nopanic.org.uk

(Information on anxiety disorders and treatments, local groups, telephone groups)

Stresswatch Scotland
Tel: 01563 574144
Helpline: 01563 528910 (Mon–Fri 10am–6pm)
Website: www.stresswatchscotland.org
Email: office@StresswatchScotland.org

(Information on stress, coping strategies, anxiety disorders and self-help groups)

Triumph Over Phobia (TOP) UK
PO Box 344
Bristol BS34 8ZR
Tel: 01225 330353
Website: www.triumphoverphobia.com
Email: triumphoverphobia@blueyonder.co.uk

(Information on obsessive compulsive disorder and phobia, self-help groups)

Adjustment disorders and acute stress reaction

Adjustment disorders

Adjustment disorders are significant emotional or behavioural symptoms (e.g. difficulty in sleeping, headache, chest pain, palpitations, abdominal pain) occurring in response to stressful events. The person feels over-whelmed and unable to cope. The source of stress may be a single event or a number of factors that affect the individual, the family or a group of people.

Acute stress reaction

Nearly everyone who encounters a trauma (e.g. assault, natural catastrophe) experiences stress, sometimes to a considerable degree. The symptoms are immediate (within an hour) but most people recover within a few days. Symptoms often include palpitations, sweating, shaking, restlessness, hot flushes, difficulty in breathing, hyperventilation, and tense muscles.

In severe acute stress reaction social withdrawal, reduced level of attention, overactivity or excessive grief may occur.

Resources

British Association for Counselling and Psychotherapy
BACP House
35–37 Albert Street
Rugby
Warwickshire CV21 2SG
Tel: 0870 443 5219
Website: www.bacp.co.uk
Email: information@bacp.co.uk

(Information on counsellors in the UK)

CRUSE Bereavement Care
Cruse House
126 Sheen Road
Richmond
Surrey TW9 1UR
Helpline: 020 8940 4818 (Mon–Fri 9.30am–5pm)
Website: www.crusebereavementcare.org.uk

(Information and advice on bereavement and dealing with a major personal crisis)

Relate
Herbert Gray College
Little Church Street
Rugby
Warwickshire CV21 3AP
Tel: 0845 456 1310
Website: www.relate.org.uk

(General information on psychotherapy and counselling)

Stresswatch Scotland
Tel: 01563 574144
Helpline: 01563 528910 (Mon–Fri 10am–6pm)
Website: www.stresswatchscotland.org
Email: office@StresswatchScotland.org

(Information on stress, coping strategies, anxiety disorders and self-help groups)

Victim Support
Cranmer House
39 Brixton Road
London
SW9 6DZ
Tel: 020 7735 9166
Helpline: 0845 30 30 900 (Mon–Fri 9am–9pm, weekends 9am–7pm, bank holidays 9am–5pm)
Website: www.victimsupport.org
Email: contact@victimsupport.org.uk

(Information on the effects of being a victim of crime and how to deal with it)

Dementia

Dementia is a group of diseases that affects how the brain works. There are many different types of dementia. The most common type is called Alzheimer's disease. Dementia leads to a gradual deterioration in skills. The majority of dementias are irreversible.

> Susan is 51 and has Down syndrome. She shares a flat with a friend with support from an outreach worker. Susan's friend is worried about her. She tells the outreach worker that Susan has not been doing her share of the housework, and gets irritable if reminded. She has been quite forgetful recently, for instance she went out to buy some milk and came home without it. Susan's friend is finding the situation difficult.

Dementia tends to affect older people in the general population. It is far more common in people aged over 80 years. People with intellectual disabilities are now living longer than before and we are starting to see more with dementia. Dementia is more common in people with intellectual disabilities. One group that is at particular risk is people with Down syndrome. Although some people with Down syndrome do develop dementia in their later years, this is not predictable or inevitable. Research indicates that the incidence of dementia in people with Down syndrome is similar to that of the general population except that it occurs 20–30 years earlier (in middle age).

Services for people with intellectual disabilities and dementia need to develop in order to meet the challenge of caring for these people, as this group will grow in size in coming years.

The signs and symptoms of dementia
EARLIER STAGES

- Loss of memory, especially short-term
- Loss of interest in activities
- Reduction in communication skills
- Difficulty in using the right words
- Difficulty in understanding others
- Difficulty in concentrating
- Gradual loss of self-help skills
- Wandering around aimlessly, not knowing where they are
- Depression and anxiety
- May start to have seizures or an increase if they already have epilepsy

LATER STAGES

- Personality changes
- Mood changes
- Increased seizures
- Loss of mobility
- Incontinence
- Total loss of self-help skills
- Problems with swallowing
- Physical health problems

Dementia affects everyone differently and people will show different signs and symptoms. It is sometimes difficult to pick up on the early stages of dementia in people with intellectual disabilities. This could be because carers help them by implementing routines and supporting them with day-to-day life, so the initial signs of forgetfulness and confusion may not be so evident.

Diagnosing dementia

It will often be the carers that notice a change in the person, such as that they are forgetting things or not being able to do so much for themselves any more. It is important that the carer supports the person to go to the GP. At this time nobody should jump to any conclusions, as there are lots of other things that will need to be considered before a diagnosis of dementia is made.

The first thing that will be done is to rule out any underlying medical problem or other mental health problems. For example the signs and symptoms in the earlier stages of dementia are very similar to those in depression. The person may need a blood test to see if they have any problems with their thyroid gland. This is a gland in the neck that produces hormones to control our metabolism. If it is not working properly it can produce dementia-like symptoms. People with Down syndrome are prone to thyroid problems. Also, lack of some vitamins can lead to dementia, but it is reversible with vitamin supplements. Vision and hearing may be tested, especially if the person is unable to communicate about problems in these areas.

Following this a psychologist may undertake an IQ test, to get a good picture of how the person is functioning on an intellectual level. If previous tests have been done they would be compared to see if there is any decline. Other professionals such as occupational therapists might complete assessments of skills. If after time the person continues to lose skills and to gradually deteriorate a diagnosis of dementia will be made.

How can you help the person you care for?

- If memory loss is mild, use of memory aids (e.g. writing a list, a picture diary) or reminders can be of help

- Encourage the person to make full use of their remaining abilities

- Keeping an eye on the person's ability to perform daily tasks safely, behavioural problems and general physical condition is necessary. Regularly assess risk (balancing safety and independence), especially at times of crisis

- Encourage maintenance of the person's physical health and fitness through good diet and exercise, plus swift treatment of any physical illness. Physical illness or stress can increase confusion

- The person will have great difficulty in learning new information. Avoid as much as possible places or situations which are unfamiliar for the person

- Encourage the person to make arrangements for support in the home, community or day care programmes, or residential placement. Discuss planning of legal and financial affairs

An assessment of the person's needs and your own (under the Carer's (Recognition and Services) Act 1995) can be requested from the local social services department. You may need continuing support after the person has entered residential care or even after they have passed away.

It is important that you look after your own mental health and how you are managing, especially if you look after the person alone. Consider ways to reduce stress (e.g. self-help groups, home help, day care and respite care).

Contact with other families caring for relatives with dementia may be helpful. Membership of a support group and information on dementia may help carers. Ask the GP for information about local services in addition to general advice about dementia. Information about benefits such as Attendance Allowance and Disability Living Allowance (DLA) is available from the Alzheimer's Society (see Resources section below).

Resources

The Foundation for People with Learning Disabilities has produced a training pack on Down syndrome and dementia published by BILD (more information will be found in the BILD website; see Resources section in Chapter 3 for contact details).

In 2002 the Foundation for People with Learning Disabilities published a report called 'Today and Tomorrow' which has a useful chapter on people with Down syndrome who develop dementia and other issues concerning people who are growing older with intellectual disabilities (see Resources section in Chapter 3 for contact details).

Age Concern

Helpline: 0800 0099 66 (every day 7am–7pm)
(Information and fact sheets on a wide range of issues relating to older people)

England
Astral House
1268 London Road
London SW16 4ER
Tel: 020 8675 7200
Website: www.ace.org.uk

Northern Ireland
3 Lower Crescent
Belfast BT7 1NR
Tel: 028 9024 5729
Advice line: 028 9032 5055 (Mon–Thurs 9.30am–1pm)
Website: www.ageconcernni.org

Scotland
113 Rose Street
Edinburgh EH2 3DT
Tel: 0131 220 3345
Website: www.ageconcernscotland.org.uk

Wales
Fourth Floor
1 Cathedral Road
Cardiff CF11 9SD
Tel: 029 2037 1566
Website: www.accymru.org.uk

Alzheimer's Society

Helpline: 0845 300 0336 (Mon–Fri 8.30am–6.30pm)
Website: www.alzheimers.org.uk
Email: Helpline@alzheimers.org.uk
(Information on dementia and associated issues)

England
Gordon House
10 Greencoat Place
London SW1P 1PH
Tel: 020 7306 0606

Northern Ireland
86 Eglantien Avenue
Belfast BT9 6EU
Tel: 0289 066 4100

Wales
Fourth floor
Baltic House
Mount Stuart Square
Cardiff CF10 5FH
Tel: 029 2043 1990

Association of Crossroads Care Attendants Scheme
10 Regent Place
Rugby
Warwickshire CV21 2PN
Tel: 01788 573653
Website: www.crossroads.org.uk
Email: communications@crossroads.org.uk

Carers Line
Tel: 0808 808 7777 (Mon–Fri 10am–12pm and 2pm–4pm)

(A helpline for carers to discuss any issue)

Carers National Association
20–25 Glasshouse Yard
London EC1A 4JT
Tel: 020 7490 8818
Advice line: 0345 573 369

(Advice and information on issues associated with caring)

Counsel and Care
Tyman House
16 Bonny Street
London NW1 9PG
Tel: 020 7241 8555
Helpline: 0845 300 7585 (Mon–Fri 10am–1pm)
Website: www.counselandcare.org.uk
Email: advice@counselandcare.org.uk

(Advice and help for older people)

Down's Syndrome Association
155 Mitcham Road
Tooting
London SW17 9PG
Tel: 020 8682 4001
Website: www.downs-syndrome.org.uk
Email: info@downs-syndrome.org.uk

(Information on the general needs of people with Down syndrome, includes information on dementia)

Help the Aged
Website: www.helptheaged.org.uk
(Information and fact sheets on a wide range of issues for older people)

England
207–221 Pentonville Road
London N1 9UZ
Tel: 020 7278 1114
Email: info@helptheaged.org.uk

Cymru (Wales)
12 Cathedral Road
Cardiff CF11 9LJ
Tel: 029 2024 6550
Email: infocymru@helptheaged.org.uk

Northern Ireland
Ascot House
24–30 Shaftesbury Square
Belfast
BT2 7DB
Tel: 0289 023 0666
Email: infoni@helptheaged.org.uk

Scotland
11 Granton Square
Edinburgh
EH5 1HX
Tel: 0131 551 6331
Email: infoscot@helptheaged.org.uk

Eating disorders

Lots of people experience changes in their eating habits during times of stress. For example if someone is under stress at work they might eat less and lose weight. If someone recently broke up with a partner they may eat more. When the feelings of stress have reduced eating habits usually return to normal.

However, some people can become preoccupied with food and eating. It can cause them distress and affect their day-to-day life, and in some cases can lead to severe consequences for their health. We would refer to these people as having an 'eating disorder'. There are several different types of eating disorder and they appear to be common in people with intellectual disabilities. Some conditions predispose to eating problems, e.g. people with Prader-Willi Syndrome may have the tendency to overeat.

A diagnosis of an eating disorder is made when the symptoms or signs are not a direct consequence of any other mental health (e.g. depression, drugs) or physical disorder and are out of keeping with the person's cultural background (e.g. abstaining from certain foods due to religious reasons). The diagnosis also takes into account that an adequate and balanced diet is available.

Eating disorders associated with intellectual disabilities include:

- **Pica:** repeated eating and/or mouthing of non-nutritive substances (e.g. soil, paper, hair, dust, paint chippings, faeces)

- **Excessive chewing/spitting out:** repeated excessive chewing and/or spitting out without swallowing resulting in weight loss or failure to gain weight

- **Food rumination/regurgitation:** repeated food regurgitation (bringing swallowed food back into the mouth) and/or food rumination (re-chewing swallowed food) resulting in weight loss or failure to gain weight

- **Food faddiness/food refusal:** refusal to eat an adequate and balanced dietary intake, failure to gain weight and/or loss of weight

- **Anorexia nervosa:** severe dieting, despite very low weight, distorted body image (an unreasonable belief that one is overweight), and amenorrhoea (lack of periods)

- **Bulimia:** binge-eating (eating large amounts of food in a few hours) and purging (attempts to eliminate food by self-induced vomiting, or via diuretic or laxative use)

Common features are:

- Unreasonable fear of being fat or gaining weight

- Extensive efforts to control weight (e.g. strict dieting, vomiting, use of purgatives, excessive exercise)

- Denial that weight or eating habits are a problem
- Low mood, anxiety/irritability
- Obsessional symptoms
- Relationship difficulties
- Increasing withdrawal
- School and work problems

There can be medical consequences of eating disorders, including:

- Amenorrhoea (periods stopping)
- Dental problems (tooth damage or decay)
- Muscle weakness
- Kidney stones
- Unusual hair growth
- Constipation
- Problems with regulating body temperature
- Liver dysfunction
- Dizziness and fainting

How can you help the person you care for?

A supportive carer, family and friends can make a big difference in the person's recovery. You may be able to help the person by employing some helpful strategies such as the following:

- Do not try to force the person to change if he or she is not ready. In spite of the stress and sadness caused by eating disorders try to avoid confrontation and judgement
- Do not simply state that the person's view is wrong
- Be patient and consistent
- Do not be hurt if the person does not want to discuss their treatment with you

- If appropriate try to educate the person about food and weight and help them to eat healthily. Be a good role model by adhering to healthy eating yourself and do not spend much time talking about dieting, food and weight

- Do not allow the eating disorder to run your family. Peculiar eating habits and food choices should not dominate your kitchen or family life. The person should not be responsible for what you eat, which restaurants you go to or where you go on outings and holidays

- Talk with the person about issues other than food, weight and diets. Listen to their feelings, opinions and ideas that have nothing to do with food

- Encourage the person to go out and meet new friends

- Help the person realize that they have to deal with the consequences of their actions

- Express your love and affection honestly and do not tie your caring to demands about gaining weight

Resources

Anorexia and Bulimia Care
PO Box 173
Letchworth
Herts SG6 1XQ
Tel: 0142 423 351
Website: www.anorexiabulimiacare.co.uk
Email: anorexiabulimiacare@ntlworld.com

(Information and advice, some especially for carers)

Anorexia Bulimia Careline (Northern Ireland)
Tel: 0289 061 4440

Centre for Eating Disorders, Scotland
Edinburgh Practice
3 Sciennes Road
Edinburgh EH9 1LE
Tel: 0131 668 3051
Website: www.maryhart.co.uk

Email: info@maryhart.co.uk
(Information and advice on a range of eating disorders)

Eating Disorders Association
First Floor
Wensum House
103 Prince of Wales Street
Norwich NR1 1DW
Helpline: 0845 634 1414 (Mon–Fri 8.30am–8.30pm)
Website: www.edauk.com
Email: helpmail@edauk.com

(Information and advice on eating disorders and where to get help)

Overeaters Anonymous
PO Box 19
Stretford
Manchester M32 9EB
Tel: 07000 784985
Website: www.overeatersanonymous.org

(General information)

Substance misuse

A lot of people will use coffee, alcohol or tobacco to experience pleasure, or to help with unpleasant emotional or physical feelings. Sometimes people use substances such as illegal drugs or alcohol in such amounts that they interfere with their physical and/or mental well-being and can contribute to the development of mental health problems. Substance misuse is not common in people with intellectual disabilities. When it does occur the substance is likely to be alcohol and it is likely to be someone with mild intellectual disabilities.

Reasons for substance abuse

Understanding why the individual is using the illegal drugs or alcohol is important in helping the person to change their lives. Some possible reasons are listed below:

- To change the mood and feel happier if the person is feeling low
- To reduce anxiety

- To increase confidence in social situations
- Because of peer pressure
- Because of low self-esteem
- To avoid unpleasant life problems
- For attention as a form of rebellion
- To reduce pain (emotional and physical)
- To help with sleep

How can you help the person you care for?

- Seek information about the substances that the person you care for is using and discuss with him or her treatment or management options available

- You should keep in mind that total abstinence from the substance misuse should be seen as a long-term goal. Gradual reduction in substance misuse may be a realistic goal in the short to medium term

- Help the person to think about the motivating factors (e.g. not having a hangover and feeling ill after the consumption of a lot of alcohol, making new friends and learning new things through music and sport) of stopping the use of these drugs

- Try to be supportive and encouraging of any small change or progress. Ensure that he or she is rewarded (by self, family or others) for abstinence or attempts at abstinence

- Discuss the negative effects of alcohol or other drugs on the body

- Highlight other negative effects of alcohol or other drugs (e.g. lack of money, trouble with the police, social problems such as relationship break-ups)

- Help with relapse prevention by supporting the person to identify the signs that can lead him or her to use the substance again. Some people choose to stay away from friends who also use drugs, or keep no money on them, for example. Support the person to find out what he or she can do instead as loneliness and boredom can cause relapse

- Encourage the person to learn to recognize tension and what situations cause stress so that he or she learn that they need to relax

- Relaxation techniques are useful for individuals who are trying to moderate their drinking or drug taking. Encourage the person to use these techniques to relieve tension and stress

- Encourage the person to keep their health appointments and receive professional help with their problem

- Encourage the person to talk to trusted friends or his or her clinician if day-to-day problems arise instead of turning immediately to drugs

Resources

A1 – ANON Family Groups UK and Eire

61 Great Dover Street
London SE1 4YF
Tel: 020 7403 0888
Helpline: 0141 339 8884 (24 hours)
Website: www.a1-anonuk.org.uk

(Information and leaflets on alcohol and family support)

ADFAM (Family, drugs and alcohol)

Waterbridge House
32–36 Loman Street
London SE1 0EH
Tel: 020 7928 8898
Helpline: 020 7928 8900
Website: www.adfam.org.uk
Email: admin@adfam.org.uk

(Information, leaflets etc.)

Alcoholics Anonymous

PO Box 1
Stonebow House
Stonebow
York YO1 7NJ

Tel: 01904 644026
Helpline: 0845 7697 555 (24 hours a day, every day)
Website: www.alcoholics-anonymous.org.uk

(Information, leaflets, contacts for local groups)

Alcohol Concern

32–36 Loman Street
Waterbridge House
London SE1 0EE
Tel: 020 7928 7377
Website: www.alcoholconcern.org.uk
Email: contact@alcoholconcern.org.uk

(Information, fact sheets, leaflets)

CITA

Cavendish House
Brighton Road
Waterloo
Liverpool L22 5NG
Tel: 0151 474 9626
Helpline: 0151 949 0102 (Mon–Fri 10am–1pm)
Website: www.liv.ac.uk/~csunit/community/cita.htm

(Information on tranquillizers and self-help groups)

Narcotics Anonymous, UK

UK Service Office
202 City Road
London EC1V 2PH
Tel: 020 7251 4007
Helpline: 020 7730 0009
Website: www.ukna.org
Email: helpline@ukna.org

(General information)

National Drinkline

Helpline: 0800 917 8282

(24-hour advice)

National Drugs Helpline

Tel: 0800 77 66 00 (24 hours a day, every day)

(Advice and information on services)

Release
388 Old Street
London EC1V 9LT
Tel: 020 7729 5255
Website: www.release.org.uk
Email: info@release.org.uk

(General information on drugs)

Personality disorders

The way we generally think or behave makes up our personalities. These develop throughout life. It is our personalities, as well as what we look like, that make us different from everyone else. As we come across new situations, we may adapt our behaviour or learn new ways of behaving, which will affect our personality. People with personality disorders find it difficult to adapt or learn new behaviours, as their personalities tend to be inflexible. These disorders generally develop during adolescence.

There are many different types of personality disorders, but people who have them tend to have the following characteristics:

- They have difficulty in conforming to what society would consider normal

- Often they have chaotic lifestyles

- Their behaviour might cause conflict with others

- They may appear irresponsible and demanding

- They care little for the views of others and are insensitive to the feelings of others

- They tend to learn little from experience, even if the previous experiences have caused harm to them or others

- They have difficulty in understanding that their own behaviour affects other people

- They tend to be impulsive, impatient and act for the moment

- They have difficulty in planning for the future

Due to the above, people with personality disorders find it difficult to find friends and partners. Their behaviour tends to cause them distress.

Little research has been carried out on personality disorders and people with intellectual disabilities. It is generally only possible to diagnose personality disorders in people with mild intellectual disabilities.

How can you help the person you care for?

People with personality disorder show unusual behaviour. They might be emotionally cold and not respond as expected to other people and situations. Often they may hold strange beliefs or suffer from depression. Some may self-harm or have drug or alcohol problems. Some might be in trouble with the police due to anti-social behaviour.

Being supportive and encouraging to the person often helps them to focus on the problem and develop positive qualities as well as hope for the future. Listening to his or her point of view will help in increasing self-esteem and feeling valued and accepted. It is also helpful to set clear limits in your interactions with the person (e.g. what is acceptable and what is not). This attitude often helps the person to increase their ability to trust others and gives them strength to face weaknesses.

Resources

For personality disorder resources please refer to the 'Resources' section in Chapter 1 and also see www.mentalhealth.org.uk.

Chapter 3

Services for People with Intellectual Disabilities and Mental Health Problems

Steve Hardy and Anastasia Gratsa

Key messages from this chapter

Introduction

Government policy on services

Primary Care Services

Community Mental Health Services

Community Learning Disabilities Teams

Specialist Mental Health in Learning Disabilities Services

In-patient services

Ways you can help services

Other services

Resources

Key messages from this chapter

- 'Valuing People' is the UK Government's plan to reshape and modernize services for people with intellectual disabilities, which is based on the themes of rights, choice, independence and inclusion.

- The Care Programme Approach (CPA) is the care management process for people who have mental health problems; this includes people with intellectual disabilities. Services, whether general or specialist, should be applying CPA to people with intellectual disabilities who have additional mental health problems.

- The General Practitioner (GP) is normally the first port of call if someone thinks they have a mental health problem. The GP may well refer the person on to other services.

- There are a variety of services that can offer assessment and treatment for people with intellectual disabilities and mental health problems in the community; these include:
  - Community Mental Health Teams
  - Community Learning Disabilities Teams
  - Specialist Mental Health in Learning Disabilities Teams

- A small proportion of people with intellectual disabilities and mental health problems may need to spend some time in hospital. Depending on the person's needs this may be a general mental health ward or a specialist ward for people with intellectual disabilities.

- There are a variety of other services that are open to the majority of people with intellectual disabilities, but may be especially helpful for those with mental health problems: day services, advocacy, direct payments, person-centred planning.

- Person-centred planning is a way of assisting people to work out what they want. Having a person-centred approach means making sure that everything is based on what is important to a person from his or her own point of view. Family members, carers, friends and services work in partnership with the individual. They can contribute and negotiate about what is safe, possible or desirable to improve the person's life.

continued...

...continued

> • The Government wants all people with intellectual
> disabilities to have a person-centred plan, if they want one. It
> is a plan that is totally focused on what each person wants; it
> includes their hopes and aspirations.

Introduction

This chapter will focus on current Government policy in England and Wales and the services that are available to people with intellectual disabilities who have additional mental health problems.

Historically, it was not recognized that people with intellectual disabilities could develop the same mental health problems as everyone else. This means that the mental health services for this particular group of people have generally not received the attention and funding that they deserve and require. However, with research over the last few decades indicating that people with intellectual disabilities are more at risk of developing mental health problems, the tide has begun to turn.

It should be noted that there are great variations in the type and availability of services across the United Kingdom. This chapter will provide a general overview of services.

Government policy on services

Some of the latest relevant Government policy for England and Wales includes the following:

- 'Valuing People'
- National Service Framework for Mental Health
- Care Programme Approach
- Health Action Plan

'Valuing People'

In March 2001 the Government published its White Paper 'Valuing People: A New Strategy for Learning Disability for the Twenty-First Century'. It was the first major policy document relating to the needs of people with intellectual disabilities in 30 years. It relates to England and Wales.

'Valuing People' sets out the Government's vision on how services for people with intellectual disabilities should be shaped and covers all areas of a person's life such as health, leisure, housing, employment and the needs of carers. There are four key principles that underpin the whole paper; these are:

- Rights
- Independence
- Choice
- Inclusion

'Valuing People' pays particular attention to the mental health needs of people with intellectual disabilities. Its main objectives include the following:

- Materials to promote positive mental health and information about the services should be provided in an accessible format for people with intellectual disabilities, including those from minority ethnic backgrounds

- There should be strategies for improving access to education, housing and employment, which will promote the mental well-being of individuals

- Where possible people with intellectual disabilities should use general mental health services

- If necessary, specialist staff from the intellectual disabilities service will provide support to people in crisis resolution/home treatment teams or other alternatives to hospital admission wherever possible

- People who require admission to hospital should use general mental health wards wherever possible. Each local service should have access to a specialist facility for the small number of people with intellectual disabilities who cannot be appropriately admitted to a general mental health ward.

National Service Framework for Mental Health

National Service Frameworks are part of the Government's plan to increase quality and reduce unacceptable variations in health and social services across the UK. They have been developed for priority areas such as heart disease, cancer, older people, children and mental health. Each sets out standards and targets that each NHS Trust and Social Services Department should be aiming to achieve. The Government will be monitoring services' progress.

The National Service Framework for Mental Health sets out seven standards, which are applicable to all adults of working age, including people with intellectual disabilities.

STANDARD ONE

This addresses mental health promotion and the discrimination and social exclusion associated with mental health problems.

STANDARDS TWO AND THREE

These are concerned with individuals' access to primary care services (such as the GP) for their mental health problems.

STANDARDS FOUR AND FIVE

These relate to the effectiveness of the care people receive from community and in-patient mental health services.

STANDARD SIX

This is for individuals who care for people with mental health problems.

STANDARD SEVEN

This sets out the action necessary to reduce suicide rates.

Free copies of this document can be obtained by phoning the Department of Health Response Line, which is listed at the end of this chapter.

Care Programme Approach

The Care Programme Approach (CPA) is the care management process for those in contact with specialist mental and social care services. It was first developed in 1991, to provide a framework for effective mental health care, and it aims to minimize the distress and confusion sometimes apparent for services users and their carers referred to the mental health system. The CPA has four main elements:

- Systematic arrangements for assessing the health and social needs of people accepted into specialist mental health services

- The formation of a care plan, which identifies the health and social care required from a variety of providers.

- The appointment of a care co-ordinator to keep in close touch with the person and to monitor and co-ordinate care

- Regular review and, where necessary, agreed changes to the care plan

'Valuing People' states that the CPA should be applied to people with intellectual disabilities who have mental health problems, though it should be noted that Community Learning Disabilities Services are only just beginning to develop the CPA.

There are two levels of the CPA, standard and enhanced. After the assessment the multi-disciplinary team will decide which level the person will be placed under.

STANDARD CPA

People placed on this level will be likely to:

- Require the support or intervention of one agency or discipline, for example a Community Psychiatric Nurse (CPN)

- Or require low-key support from more than one agency or mental health worker

- Be more able to manage their mental health problems on their own

- Have an informal support network (good support from friends and family)
- Pose little danger to themselves or others
- Be more likely to keep in contact with services

There is no specific the CPA paperwork but mental health professionals must keep detailed written records of assessments, care plans and reviews.

ENHANCED CPA

People placed on this level of the CPA will be those:

- Who have been in hospital under a section of the Mental Health Act (1983) for treatment
- Who require involvement and co-ordination from many different agencies
- Who have a diagnosis of severe and enduring mental health problems

There is a specific written form (Care Programme) which includes details of:

- A list of all those involved in the person's care
- Assessment (including risk assessment)
- Care plans
- Side effects of medication
- What to do in case of an emergency

The person is allocated someone to work as a care co-ordinator. The care co-ordinator is responsible for ensuring the care programme is put into practice and regularly reviewed.

All those involved in the CPA, including the person and their carer, will receive a copy of the plan.

Health Action Plan

The Health Action Plan (HAP) is the Government's new initiative (arising from 'Valuing People') that aims to ensure that all people with intellectual disabilities have their health needs met. It includes details of:

- The need for health interventions
- Oral health and dental care
- Fitness and mobility
- Continence
- Vision and hearing
- Nutrition
- Emotional needs
- Details of medication taken and side effects
- Records of any screening tests

Each person will have a health facilitator, who will co-ordinate the HAP.

Some people with intellectual disabilities who have mental health problems will fall under the umbrella of the Care Programme Approach (CPA). Part of the CPA addresses the person's health needs. You can help with this if appropriate and ensure that the focus is on the general health needs (not just the mental health) of the person you care for. The intention is that the CPA will be the HAP for this group of people, and their CPA care co-ordinator will also be their health facilitator.

Services for people with intellectual disabilities and mental health problems

The following provide services for people with intellectual disabilities and mental health problems:

- Primary Care Services
- Community Mental Health Teams
- Crisis Resolution/Home Treatment Teams
- Assertive Outreach Teams

- Community Learning Disabilities Teams
- Specialist Mental Health in Learning Disabilities Services

Primary Care Services

For most of us the first service we will visit if we think we have a mental health problem is our General Practitioner (GP), unless it is an emergency situation, then we might visit or be taken to an accident and emergency department.

For someone with intellectual disabilities who is already known to mental health, intellectual disabilities or specialist services, they would probably not have to visit their GP for their mental health needs. The person you care for, or you on their behalf, would contact the professional they already have contact with.

GPs form part of what is known as 'Primary Care Services'. This basically means they are the first port of call for people. This also includes health clinics, such as Well Woman and Man clinics. Primary care professionals are able to offer assessment and treatment, but also they are the gateway for people to use other specialist services.

GPs are able to assess and treat a wide range of mental health problems, but these problems tend to be mild in nature. For example a GP may prescribe antidepressants to someone with mild depression and refer them to a counsellor to discuss their problems. However, with someone who has more complex needs and what appears to be a more severe and/or enduring mental health problem, they would most likely refer them to a community mental health, intellectual disabilities or specialist service.

Whether the person with intellectual disabilities was referred to a mental health, intellectual disabilities or specialist service would really depend on service developments within the area and the GP's awareness of them.

Community Mental Health Services

Community Mental Health Teams (CMHTs) are what we call general services. Any adult of working age who has a mental health problem can access them. There will be at least one in every borough or district within the UK. They are based in the community, generally at an easily accessible location. The Community Mental Health Team is a multi-disciplinary team that works together to assess, treat and support the person with a mental health problem. The following professionals usually work there:

- Psychiatrists
- Clinical psychologists
- Community psychiatric nurses (CPNs)
- Social workers
- Occupational therapists (OTs)

The most common way to gain access to a Community Mental Health Team is by referral from a GP.

People with intellectual disabilities and mental health problems will generally be referred to a Community Mental Health Team in the following circumstances:

- If they have mild intellectual disabilities and a mental health problem
- If the local Community Learning Disabilities Team does not have any staff specializing in mental health problems
- If there is no Specialist Mental Health in Learning Disabilities Team
- If the Community Mental Health Team staff member feels they have the skills and knowledge to provide effective care to the person with intellectual disabilities

Once a referral has been received a member of the team will see the person to start the assessment process. People may see health professionals either at the Community Mental Health Team or at their home. They will assess the person's current needs and state of mental health. Depending on the individual's needs they may refer them to another professional in the team for additional work, such as an occupational therapist or clinical psychologist.

Community Mental Health Teams will provide care under the CPA framework. This means that the person's needs will be discussed at a team meeting and the team will decide on the most suitable member of the team to be the care co-ordinator. A care plan will be written, involving all those involved in the person's care, including you and the person you care for. The care co-ordinator will regularly meet with you and the person you care for to monitor progress.

Assessment and treatment packages will be holistic in nature, which means they will take into consideration many aspects of the person's life and look at what impact these have on their mental health. The care package may well involve professionals from other organizations such as education, housing and employment. This will depend on the person's individual needs.

Members of the Community Mental Health Team
PSYCHIATRIST

A psychiatrist is a trained doctor who after doing their medical training specialized in mental health. Their role is to assess, diagnose, treat and manage mental health problems. Working as part of the multi-disciplinary team they develop holistic intervention plans. A psychiatrist working in a Community Mental Health Team has also specialized in the mental health needs of adults of working age. There will be several psychiatrists working in a team:

- A consultant psychiatrist, who is fully qualified and has specialized in a particular area
- Junior doctors:
  - Specialist registrars (SpRs) who are psychiatrists but are training to specialize in a particular area
  - Senior house officers (SHOs), qualified doctors who are training to become psychiatrists

CLINICAL PSYCHOLOGIST

Clinical psychologists aim to reduce psychological distress and to enhance and promote psychological well-being. In mental health teams the clinical psychologist will help people experiencing distress by using talking therapies such as cognitive behavioural therapy and other therapies as described in Chapter 4 on therapeutic interventions. They will work with the person you care for and yourself, to help solve problems.

COMMUNITY PSYCHIATRIC NURSE

Community psychiatric nurses (CPNs) are Registered Mental Nurses who work in the community. They will work as part of the multi-disciplinary team to assess mental health problems and work out appropriate interventions. CPNs will support the person in getting treatment at home. One of their main roles will be to monitor the effectiveness and possible side effects of medication and to provide support and education to the person you care for, yourself, and other members of the family. Some CPNs have been trained to deliver psychological interventions such as counselling and cognitive behavioural therapy.

SOCIAL WORKER

A social worker is a professional who works as part of the multi-disciplinary team. Their main role is to assess how the person's social situation is contributing to and impacting on their mental health problem. They will then work out a package of care to improve the situation. This may include looking at the person's housing, employment, recreation and help with receiving the appropriate benefits. Some social workers in the Community Mental Health Team have completed extra training on the Mental Health Act (1983); they are called approved social workers (ASWs). An approved social worker can assess an individual to see if they need to be detained under the Mental Health Act to receive treatment.

OCCUPATIONAL THERAPIST[1]

An occupational therapist (OT) will assess how the individual's mental health problems have had an effect on their ability to do everyday things. They will work out interventions that aim to maximize the level of functioning and independence in all aspects of life. The occupational therapist assesses the physical, psychological and social functions of the person, identifies areas where there are problems, and involves the person in a structured programme of activity to help overcome their problems. The activities selected will relate to the person's personal, social, cultural and economic needs and will reflect the environmental factors which are important in his or her life. Occupational therapists may work with the person individually or get them involved in groups, such as relaxation groups for those with anxiety.

Crisis Resolution / Home Treatment Teams

Often, going into a mental health ward can be a very distressing experience. Within the NHS there is also a great pressure on the mental health in-patient wards for beds. With this in mind the Government has started to develop Crisis Resolution and Home Treatment Teams. They are not available in each area as yet, but there are plans to extend the services.

These teams are operational 24 hours a day, 7 days a week. They offer a rapid response to people who are in crisis, usually within an hour. They are multi-disciplinary, but mental health nurses, who are supported by psychiatrists, mainly staff them. Their main aim is to resolve crises within the person's own home and to try and prevent hospital admission.

To find out if there is such a team in your local area, contact your local mental health NHS Trust or GP.

Assertive Outreach Teams

There are a number of people living in the community who have severe mental health problems. Some of these people are at risk of losing contact with mental health services and of relapse. This group of people often have more than one problem, such as severe mental illness with drug abuse. They often have repeated admissions into hospital.

The Government has developed Assertive Outreach Teams to work with this group. They are multi-disciplinary teams that work outside of the normal working hours. The team works intensively with the person and their carers. People are not allocated a key worker, as the whole team is the person's key worker.

Assertive Outreach Teams are relatively new and are not established in each area. To find out if there is a team in your local area, contact your local mental health NHS Trust or GP.

Community Learning Disabilities Teams

Community Learning Disabilities Teams (CLDTs) are multi-disciplinary teams that provide assessment, intervention and develop care packages for the health care and social care management of people with intellectual disabilities. They generally consist of:

- Social workers/care managers
- Community nurses
- Clinical psychologists
- Physiotherapists
- Occupational therapists
- Psychiatrists
- Speech and language therapists
- Challenging behaviour workers

The Community Learning Disabilities Team has traditionally provided direct specialist health care and social care management for people with intellectual disabilities living in the community. The Government wants the teams to refocus in line with the values set out in the White Paper 'Valuing People'. They will now also:

- Take on a health facilitation role by helping people access general health services, both in-patient and out-patient
- Provide specialist support and expertise to the staff working in general services
- Teach staff from social services and the independent sector to become more familiar with how to support people with intellectual disabilities to have their health needs met

In terms of the mental health needs of people with intellectual disabilities, the Community Learning Disabilities Team will address them if they have a psychiatrist within the team. Some areas will have a separate specialist mental health in intellectual disabilities team, which is described later. Within some Community Learning Disabilities Teams community nurses have completed specialized training in the mental health needs of people with intellectual disabilities and will work closely with the psychiatrist.

Members of the Community Learning Disabilities Team
SOCIAL WORKERS/CARE MANAGERS

These are professionals who will provide community care assessments for people with intellectual disabilities, to identify what their needs are and to develop a care package to meet those needs within the available resources. The care package may include the use of day services, employment schemes, special education for adults, residential care, supported housing, travel passes, sorting out an electricity bill, or disability living allowance. Social workers/care managers are responsible for providing care management services under the Community Care Act (1990). They commission a package of services for their client and they are responsible for reviewing and monitoring it. A social worker is a professional who has a recognized qualification in social work. Some Community Learning Disabilities Teams will employ care managers, who will do the same job as a social worker but do not necessarily have a social work qualification. They may have other qualifications, such as occupational therapists or nurses.

COMMUNITY NURSES

These are Registered Nurses in Learning Disabilities (RNLD, previously RNMH). They will assess and develop care plans to meet the health needs of individuals. Particular areas that they may specialize in are sexual health, continence and epilepsy. A big part of their role is promoting healthy living.

CLINICAL PSYCHOLOGISTS

Clinical psychologists in Community Learning Disabilities Teams will do similar work to those who work in the Community Mental Health Teams, such as working out interventions to reduce distress and promote psychological well-being. However, in Community Learning Disabilities Teams they may also work with people whose behaviour is challenging and try to find out why people are behaving in particular ways. They may be asked to assess people to see if they are eligible to use learning disabilities services. Sometimes they will assess a person's capacity to give consent, for example if they needed an operation. They also work with staff members (e.g. in residential care homes).

PHYSIOTHERAPISTS[2]

A physiotherapist is a health care professional who is concerned with human functioning and movement. They will use a wide range of treatment techniques to restore movement and function within the body. Their work may include teaching people various exercises to help maintain mobility.

OCCUPATIONAL THERAPISTS

An occupational therapist (OT) will assess how the individual's disability affects their ability to do everyday things. They will devise interventions that aim to maximize the level of functioning and independence in all aspects of life. Interventions may include teaching the person new skills, such as cooking for themselves. They will also assess the person's environment and recommend changes to enhance the level of functioning, such as introducing aids and adaptations.

PSYCHIATRISTS

The psychiatrist in the Community Learning Disabilities Team will do similar work to those that work in the Community Mental Health Team, but they have specialized in the mental health needs of people with intellectual disabilities.

SPEECH AND LANGUAGE THERAPISTS[3]

Speech and language therapists are specialists in communication disorders. They work to assess, diagnose and develop programmes of care to maximize a person's communication. They also work with people who have swallowing, eating and drinking difficulties. The speech and language therapist will work directly with the person who has communication difficulties but will also be involved in working with those around them. Such work might involve teaching carers sign language or introducing alternative means of communication such as visual timetables.

CHALLENGING BEHAVIOUR WORKERS

These are staff that concentrate on working with people whose behaviour is challenging. They will work closely with carers, looking at the causes and functions of the challenging behaviour and develop interventions to reduce the challenging behaviour and replace it with more appropriate constructive behaviour. It should be noted that some Community Learning Disabilities Teams do not have these workers; in those instances the psychologists may work with the people that need this service.

Specialist Mental Health in Learning Disabilities Services

In some areas across the UK specialist teams have been developed that specifically focus on the mental health needs of people with learning disabilities (sometimes referred to as MHiLD teams). These teams are multi-disciplinary and based in the community.

The Mental Health in Learning Disabilities teams provide two major functions: the first is a clinical function and the second is service related. Clinically they provide specialist assessment and treatment, which may be home based or at an out-patient clinic. On a service level they may provide advice and consultation to other services and training, especially to care staff.

One example of such a team is the specialist mental health in learning disability service that operates in South East London. It has the same characteristics as other specialist teams: a clear definition of the mental health problems people with intellectual disabilities might have (based for example on diagnosis, age or gender); an explicit range of treatments; a fixed capacity and well-clarified roles and responsibilities with high levels of specialized training and skill among their staff team. People are referred to this service from GPs or other community mental health teams.

The clinical team consists of psychiatrists and community psychiatric nurses. It also works with clinical psychologists, challenging needs practitioners (specializing mainly in behaviour analysis), occupational therapists, speech therapists and social workers. This team works closely with other local mental health services, local specialist intellectual disabilities teams, and health and social care services. It provides out-patient clinics, outreach work, in-patient assessment and treatment, and consultation with community agencies for people with intellectual disabilities and mental health problems. It also provides training to care providers.

There are three phases in the provision of clinical services: structured assessment, intervention and follow-up. Therapeutic interventions are based on multi-disciplinary work and include biological interventions, psychological interventions such as cognitive behavioural therapy and social interventions such as making changes to the person's environment or social circumstances (see Chapter 4 on therapeutic interventions). Crisis prevention plans are developed to help families and service providers identify early signs of breakdown and to take appropriate action. Weekly team meetings are held to review progress. Training is offered to families and caregivers at this stage, to help them better understand and respond to the mental health needs of people with intellectual disabilities. This may take the form of seminars, books or videos, as well as modelling and role-playing exercises. Ongoing support and consultation is also provided. Follow-up is provided for as long as required. Once the person appears stable and the agreed upon care plan seems effective the team maintains quarterly or six-monthly contact.

In-patient services

The vast majority of people with intellectual disabilities who have mental health problems receive treatment in the community. However, some will require a more structured and controlled environment in which their mental health problems can be assessed and treated. The person will be more likely to be admitted into hospital if:

- They have a severe mental health problem
- They do not recognize that they are unwell
- They are refusing assessment and treatment
- They are presenting with serious risks, such as causing harm to themselves or others
- They or their carers are unable to cope at home

In-patient services include:

- General in-patient services
- Specialist intellectual disabilities in-patient services

General in-patient services

Every health district within the UK will have at least one in-patient ward for adults with mental health problems. These wards are for anybody who is an adult of working age. They are normally based on a general hospital site and are staffed by mental health nurses, with daily support from psychiatrists and occupational therapists. Each ward will generally have 15 to 20 people staying there. Whilst on the ward people will be assessed and then a treatment plan will be implemented. Each person will be allocated a psychiatrist and a named nurse. The named nurse is responsible for ensuring the care plans are written, implemented and reviewed. People on the ward may or may not be detained under the Mental Health Act (1983).

In-patient services have close links with Community Mental Health Teams and each person on the ward will be allocated a community worker for when they are discharged (if they do not already have one).

One of the main aims of 'Valuing People' is that people with intellectual disabilities will use general health services wherever possible, and this includes in-patient services. People with intellectual disabilities who need to be admitted into hospital are more likely to use general in-patient services if they have mild intellectual disabilities.

Specialist intellectual disabilities in-patient services

It is recognized that general in-patient services will not be suitable for everyone who has intellectual disabilities and requires hospital admission for their mental health problems. These people will generally have one or more of the following characteristics:

- They have difficulty in communicating their needs
- They are vulnerable
- They are easily suggestible
- They have strict routines and rituals
- Their behaviour is severely challenging
- They have complex needs that need specialist multi-disciplinary input
- They need specialist monitoring of medication
- They require a longer stay

These people are more likely to use specialist in-patient services for people with intellectual disabilities. Specialist in-patient services may be called many different names such as assessment and treatment units or intensive support units, but they will generally serve the same purpose. These services are usually smaller than general wards and are not necessarily based on a hospital site. They are staffed by nurses, both mental health and intellectual disabilities trained, with daily support from psychiatrists and occupational therapists. Each person on the ward will be assessed and an appropriate treatment package devised and implemented. The length of stay for the person will vary depending on the complexity of needs. People on the ward may or may not be detained under the Mental Health Act (1983).

Unfortunately not every local area has such a service, and even those that do appear not to have enough beds. Due to this there are a significant number of people with intellectual disabilities with mental health problems living in specialist in-patient units miles away from the person's home and family.

Ways you can help services

Regardless of what service the person you care for is referred to, they will in part follow a similar framework. Staff and professionals within the service will need to collect information about the person you care for, their problems, their history and their current situation. There are several things that you can do to aid this process. (Please see section on Mental Health Assessment in Chapter 1.)

When talking to social workers or social services departments on behalf of the person you care for, it is advisable to have the person's national insurance number, date of birth and NHS number available. This will save you time and will enable the professional to access information faster.

Other services

The following services are available to the majority of people with intellectual disabilities, whether or not they have additional mental health problems. They are described here as the use of such services may well play a part in the care of those with mental health problems and help maintain the positive mental health of others. Social workers and/or care managers should be able to provide detailed information on where you can get these services.

- Direct Payments
- Person-centred planning
- Advocacy
- Housing and planning for the future
- Respite services or short-term breaks
- Day and employment services

Direct Payments

Direct Payments allow people (including people with intellectual disabilities) in receipt of community care services to receive money, which they can use to purchase their own services. Social services departments are responsible for running Direct Payments schemes, and social workers/care managers will have information to help.

The Government are keen to promote Direct Payments, as they are an effective way of supporting greater choice and control for people with intellectual disabilities, though research in 2000 by the Social Services Inspectorate has shown that not many people with intellectual disabilities have used them; in the study only 216 out of 3700 people in receipt of Direct Payments were those with a learning disability.

People can receive a direct payment to purchase support for some of their assessed needs and continue to receive services from the local authority to meet other assessed needs.

Examples of people using Direct Payments include:

- A young woman with intellectual disabilities wanted to further her education but needed extra support to go to the adult education centre. She received a direct payment to pay for an agency support worker to take her twice a week

- A man, who lived at home with his mother, was feeling quite isolated and bored. He had tried going to the local day centre but did not really enjoy it. He used Direct Payments to pay for a support worker to take him to the leisure centre once a week and bowling every other week.

Person-centred planning
WHO WILL CREATE THE PLAN?

Person-centred planning is a way of assisting people to work out what they want, what sort of support they require and helping them get it in their communities. Having a person-centred approach means making sure that everything is based on what is important to a person from his or her own point of view. Person-centred planning is not the same as assessment and care planning. It is not concerned with eligibility for resources or other predetermined criteria. It is applicable and useful for anyone regardless of ability or cultural background. Person-centred planning is one of the key elements from 'Valuing People' and the Government wants everybody with intellectual disabilities in England and Wales to have a person-centred plan, though this will take a while and they have prioritized the following people:

- People still living in long-stay hospitals
- Young people moving from children's to adults' services
- People using large day centres
- People living in the family home with carers aged over 70
- People living in NHS residential campuses

Person-centred planning has five features that distinguish it from other forms of planning:

1. *The person is at the centre.* Person-centred planning is rooted in the principles of rights, independence and choice. It requires careful listening about how a person wants to live and what support they need.

2. *Family members and friends work in full partnership with services.* Person-centred planning puts people in the context of their family and communities. Friends and families can be valued for their contributions and negotiate conflicts about what is safe, possible or desirable to improve the person's life.

3. *Person-centred planning reflects the person's capacities.* It specifies the support the person requires to make a valued contribution to their community. Services are delivered in the context of the life a person chooses and are not about slotting people into 'gaps'.

4. *Person-centred planning builds a shared commitment to action that recognizes the person's rights.* It is an ongoing process of working together to make changes that the person and those close to them agree will improve quality of life.

5. *Person-centred planning leads to continual listening, learning and action and helps the person get what they want out of life.* Learning from planning can not only inform individuals but can also affect service delivery as a whole and inform and inspire others to achieve greater things.

Advocacy

> Effective advocacy can transform the lives of people with learning disabilities by enabling them to express their wishes and aspirations and make real choices.
>
> 'Valuing People', Department of Health (2001)

There are two main forms of advocacy:

- *Self advocacy*: this is where people with intellectual disabilities speak for themselves and say 'yes' or 'no' because they want to. It's about making your own choices, even if you might make mistakes

- *Citizen advocacy:* this is where a person, who is a volunteer, is prepared to commit to a long-term relationship with someone with intellectual disabilities and seek to understand and represent that person's views such as in care planning meetings

The amount of self and citizen advocacy services across the UK has been patchy over recent years, but the Government is driving forward the promotion of these services and has recently made extra funding available for service development.

Advocacy services are especially important for people with intellectual disabilities who have additional mental health problems. They are doubly disadvantaged and may face discrimination and the reality of not being listened to.

To find out if there is a self or citizen advocacy service you can contact the social worker/care manager or Community Learning Disabilities Team that you deal with.

Housing and planning for the future

In 2002 Mencap carried out a national survey of all local authorities in England in order to find out how many people lived with older carers, and what the future needs were of people with intellectual disabilities living with their families or carers aged over 60 and over 70. The results of the survey showed that half of the local authorities do not know how many people are living with older parents aged 70 or over. Also, the shortage of housing and support places (outside the family home) for people with intellectual disabilities is worrying. Existing provisions will not meet increasing demands as people with intellectual disabilities live longer. In 'Valuing People', it is stated that people with intellectual disabilities and their families should be able to plan for the future in good time so that parents and families do not have to face uncertainty in old age and so that their sons and daughters gain independence in a planned way. It is a priority to find alternative accommodation for people living with older parents aged 70 and over.

LIVING ALONE

This is also called independent living or supported living. The person can rent a house or flat through a housing association, the council or a landlord. Some people with intellectual disabilities have chosen to buy their home. This does not mean that the people have to be able to do every-thing for themselves; they may have a support worker who comes into the house a few hours a day or week to help out. Some people have used Direct Payments to employ their own staff and supporters.

Some people live in supported living with one or two others. It is possible that a person with high support needs can live in his or her own tenancy.

LIVING WITH A GROUP

Residential care is for people who require a lot of support at home. This type of care is generally provided by voluntary organizations (charities or trusts), private organizations and occasionally social services. Some NHS trusts provide a limited amount of residential accommodation, but the Government wants to reduce these services, as the vast majority of people with intellectual disabilities require social care as opposed to 24-hour health care.

The homes will generally be staffed by social care staff, unless they are in NHS accommodation, where some nurses will be employed. The aims of such homes vary according to individual need but generally they aim to support people to become as independent as possible, to become part of their local community and provide a good quality of life.

LIVING WITH A FAMILY

The person with intellectual disabilities will be placed with a family. The family provides as much or as little support as required by the person. This is also called adult placement or supported lodging. The person usually has their own room but they share the rest of the house with the other family members.

LIVING IN SHELTERED HOUSING OR CLUSTER HOUSING OR LIVING
SUPPORT NETWORKS

These are all terms for groups of homes (flats or houses), which are near each other in the same area. There is usually a warden or support worker who can help with getting benefits or paying bills. The person is responsible for his or her own cooking, housework and shopping.

Respite services or short-term breaks

Some areas will provide respite care services, where people with intellectual disabilities may stay every now and then for a few days or up to a few weeks. They are generally based in the community and are managed either by social services or by a private/voluntary organization. They are based on the same philosophy as group homes and they try to maintain the individual's normal routine as much as possible, such as attending a day service or college. You can contact the social worker/care manager that you deal with to see if your area has such a service.

Day and employment services

These can be provided by statutory services (usually social services, though the NHS does operate a limited amount for people with severe challenging behaviour) or the voluntary sector. Day services offer support to adults with a wide range of intellectual disabilities and they are also important to carers as they provide breaks from the caring role. They can operate as drop-in centres or provide long-term support. People have the opportunity to meet socially and receive practical support individually or in group sessions.

The main aims of such centres are to enable those who attend to achieve their maximum potential by providing intellectual opportunities to support each person's development. The Government wants to refocus day services, modernizing them so they provide new opportunities that are individually focused. They want them to help to integrate people into the community, and focus more on helping people to find education, employment and work opportunities. One of the objectives from 'Valuing People' is that day services will be modernized by 2006. Day services provide a range of services such as:

- Life skills assessment and training

- Therapeutic activities such as music, art, sensory activities and reminiscence

- Therapy groups such as anger management, assertiveness techniques, art therapy, dramatherapy

- Work orientation, meaningful occupation, sheltered employment projects and work experience placements in the community

- Training opportunities to help people find employment

- Leisure activities, for example horse riding and swimming

- Training on skills such as using computers, horticulture

Throughout the UK are some services that specifically help people with intellectual disabilities look for employment and then support them with their jobs.

Notes

1   For more information see the College of Occupational Therapists website: www.cot. co.uk

2   For more information see the Chartered Society of Physiotherapy website: www.csp. co.uk

3   For more information see the Royal College of Speech and Language Therapists website: www.rcslt.org

Resources

Benefits Enquiry Line
Tel: 0800 882200

(Information on Disability Living Allowance (care component) and Invalid Care Allowance)

British Institute of Learning Disabilities (BILD)
Campion House
Green Street
Kidderminster
Worcestershire DY10 1JL
Tel: 01562 723010
Fax: 01562 723029
Website: www.bild.org.uk
Email: enquiries@bild.org.uk

(A not-for-profit organization. It provides information, fact sheets, publications and training and consultancy services for organizations and individuals.)

British Psychological Society
St Andrews House
48 Princess Road East
Leicester LE1 7DR
Tel: 0116 254 9568
Website: www.bps.org.uk

Chartered Society of Physiotherapy
14 Bedford Row
London WC1R 4ED
Tel: 020 7306 6611
Website: www.csp.org.uk

Circles Network UK
Potford's Dam Farm
Coventry Road
Cawston, Rugby
Warwickshire CV23 9JP
Tel: 01788 816 671
Fax: 01788 816 672
Website: www.circlesnetwork.org.uk

(For support, advice and information about inclusion and circles of support)

College of Occupational Therapists
106–114 Borough High Street
Southwark
London SE1 1LB
Tel: 020 7357 6480
Website: www.cot.co.uk

Department of Health: Learning Disabilities
Website: www.dh.gov.uk/policyandguidance/healthandsocialcaretopics/
learningdisabilities/fs/en

Department of Health: Mental Health
Website: www.dh.gov.uk/policyandguidance/healthandsocialcaretopics/
mentalhealth/fs/en

(Copies of the National Services Framework for Mental Health are available from the
website or hard copies can be ordered from Ordering Publications, Department of
Health, PO Box 777, London SE1 6XH, or telephone 08701 555 455

Estia
Estia Centre
Munro – Guy's Hospital
66 Snowsfields
London SE1 3SS
Tel: 020 7378 3218
Website: www.estiacentre.org

First Step
First Floor
32–34 Hare Street
Woolwich
London SE18 6LZ
Tel: 020 8855 7886
Website: www.fst.org.uk
Email: firststep@fst.org.uk

(Developing work projects for people with mental health problems and other disadvantages)

Foundation for People with Learning Disabilities
Website: www.fpld.org.uk

England
83 Victoria Street
London SW1H 0HW
Tel: 020 7802 0300
Fax: 020 7802 0301
Email: fpld@fpld.org.uk

Scotland
Merchants House
30 George Square
Glasgow G2 1EG
Tel: 0141 572 0125
Fax: 0141 572 0246
Email: Scotland@mhf.org.uk

Housing Options
78a High Street
Witney
Oxfordshire OX8 6HL
Tel: 01993 776318
Website: www.housingoptions.org.uk
Email: enquiries@housingoptions.org.uk

(Offers housing advice for people with intellectual disabilities, families and supporters)

Jobcentre Plus
Website: www.jobcentreplus.gov.uk

(Help and advice on job hunting and extra support, and on making a claim for benefit)

Mencap
123 Golden Lane
London EC1Y 0RT
Website: www.mencap.org.uk

England
Learning Disabilities Helpline: 0808 808 1111 (free phone)
Email: help@mencap.org.uk

Wales
Learning Disabilities Helpline: 0808 8000 300 (free phone)
Email: wales@mencap.org.uk

The National Centre for Independent Living (NCIL)
250 Kennington Lane
London SE11 5RD
Tel: 020 7587 1663
Website: www.ncil.org.uk

(Focuses specifically on the implementation of Direct Payments)

Royal College of Nursing
Head Office
20 Cavendish Square
London W1G 0RN
Tel: 020 7409 3333
Website: www.rcn.org.uk

Royal College of Psychiatrists
National Headquarters
17 Belgrave Square
London SW1X 8PG
Tel: 020 7235 2351
Website: www.rcpsych.ac.uk

Royal College of Speech and Language Therapists
2 White Hart Yard
London SE1 1NX
Tel: 020 7378 1200
Website: www.rcslt.org

Values into Action (VIA)
Oxford House
Derbyshire Street
London E2 6HG
Tel: 020 7729 5436
Website: www.viauk.org

(Campaigns with people who have intellectual difficulties to eradicate discrimination against them and to ensure that their rights as human beings are respected)

Valuing People Support Team
Email: valuing.people.info@doh.qsi.gov.uk
Website: www.valuingpeople.gov.uk

Chapter 4

Therapeutic Interventions

Anastasia Gratsa, Geraldine Holt and Steve Hardy

Key messages from this chapter

- Many people with mental health problems receive help from a variety of professionals including doctors, nurses, occupational therapists and clinical psychologists. A thorough assessment is necessary to decide upon the most suitable management plan.
- Mental health problems have biological, psychological and social components. Just as physical, psychological and social factors working together contribute to the development of a mental health problem, various physical, psychological and social

continued...

...continued

interventions are available to treat a mental health problem. There are three main ways in which to help people with mental health problems:

- ○ Biological interventions: different drugs aim to correct different chemical imbalances, which in turn have a beneficial effect on behaviour. Newer drugs cause fewer unwanted effects.

- ○ Psychological interventions: different psychological therapies help the person to deal with their feelings. Referrals are accepted from GPs or mental health professionals.

- ○ Social interventions: different social interventions aim to change the person's environment or social circumstances.

- Interventions should be designed in the light of an assessment. The intensity of the programme and approach (whether group-work, individual programmes, or combinations of both) will be determined by the findings of this assessment. Also, techniques that match the level of understanding and preferred approach of each person involved are used (e.g. pictures, modelling, role-playing, etc.).

- Carers can help with interventions in the home setting if agreed by the person and the clinician. A range of interventions can be used to suit the person and the carers.

- Carers often act as advocates by helping individuals to make important decisions about management plans.

Introduction

A therapeutic intervention, also known as simply an intervention, can be any form of treatment, such as medication, counselling, or moving to improved accommodation. Interventions aim to cure an illness or at least reduce the suffering and make it more manageable. This chapter outlines the different types of biological, psychological and social interventions used for mental health problems in people with intellectual disabilities.

A carer explains her way of coping over the years. She also talks about age appropriateness in her own words. The person whom she cares for has intellectual disabilities and behaviour problems.

> You have to be very, very tolerant. You have to break everything down into tiny steps that a child can understand. When he was tiny he could write but it would be one long line, no gaps, and I would say to him every time you write a word, put your finger, and then start the next word and put your finger again. I explained that to the teacher at the school and she said yes, that is a good idea. I was so proud when he did a whole page. I have kept that page still to this day. The headmaster put on it well done! You know well done! I am really pleased that you have done a whole page of writing and then the teacher took him out the next day because he had done a whole page of writing. I thought yes, praise him, give him that little bit of confidence!
>
> Sometimes I have to do things my way because I know it works. Sometimes I will say no you have not behaved. Other times I will go out and buy little things and he will say thanks a lot because it's a reward, he doesn't realize I am rewarding him, they are little things but he really enjoys that. I know it sounds horrible being sly, but you have to be like that because that is the only way they understand. I say you be good, behave and I will get you something. He says you are treating me like a baby. But you are not treating him like a baby you are treating him like his age group, for what his age is. He is 26, his body is 26 but his age is maybe 10, maybe a bit older. I am not sure because I am not a doctor but that is the age group to me. So when he acts like he is only 10, I treat him that way and then when he acts like he is 26, I treat him like he is 26. It is helpful to him as well as he can understand better that way. It is tough at times, really tough, but we will get there in the end.

The mental health assessment process

Mental health professionals must complete an assessment with the person in order to decide what the problem is and to decide on the best therapeutic intervention to use.

Before any mental health assessment or therapeutic intervention is made it is important that a person's informed consent is sought. See Chapter 6 on 'Law, Policy and Ethical Issues' for a discussion around consent.

A thorough assessment may mean the difference between success and failure of any plan. For example, an interview with the person who exhibits challenging behaviour might reveal that the undesirable behaviour occurs at certain times of the day. Observing the person directly around those times might reveal what makes that behaviour happen. This will then help for developing strategies to be used to make the behaviour less likely to happen again.

Physical, psychological and social factors working together can contribute to the development of a mental health problem (see also Chapter 1 for a discussion on mental health assessments). In the same way various physical, psychological and social interventions are available to treat these mental health problems. Whatever methods are chosen they should reflect the needs and wishes of the person who is having the therapy. The person you care for should be involved as much as possible throughout the process.

What are therapeutic interventions?

If someone has a mental health problem a **therapeutic intervention** may be suggested to help the person cope with illness and to make it better. For example if someone has depression a GP or psychiatrist might prescribe him or her some medication, or suggest counselling.

Most professionals believe that all illness has biological, psychological and social components. Possible examples of these components are given below for the illness tuberculosis:

- The **biological** component: infection with bacteria and the person's level of immunity

- The **psychological** component: the way the person reacts emotionally to their illness; for instance, do they go to see the doctor as soon as they realize they are ill, do they want to take tablets, etc.

- The **social** component: the person's housing situation that has resulted in conditions where tuberculosis is likely to thrive

The same is true for mental health problems. They also have biological, psychological and social components. Many people with mental health problems receive help from a variety of professionals including doctors, nurses, social workers, occupational therapists and clinical psychologists, and between them they are able to look at all of these important components.

There are three main ways in which to help people with mental health problems:

- **Biological therapies:** medication which acts on the physical or biological aspects of the problem

- **Psychological therapies** which help the person to deal with their feelings

- **Social therapies** that aim to change the person's environment or social circumstances

Therapeutic interventions can include biological interventions, psychological interventions and social interventions.

Biological interventions

Biological interventions for mental health problems consist of medication. There are many different types of medications that can be used for mental health problems. These are sometimes referred to as psychotropic medication. Different types are described later in this chapter. First of all some information is provided about:

- The names of medication

- The different forms of medication

- Why medications are prescribed

- Why side effects can occur

- What you need to ask professionals about medication

- What you need to watch out for

- What information you should get from the doctor or nurse

- How the medication will be monitored

Names of medication

Medications have two or more names and they can be difficult to pronounce. One is the chemical name (from the compound it is made from) and the others are brand names (given to them by the companies that make them). For example:

Chemical name: Chlorpromazine

Brand name: Largactil

What form do medications come in?

Medication can come as a tablet, capsule, liquid to drink, or as an injection. Most people will be prescribed tablets and they are likely to be taken at least once a day. Sometimes doctors will prescribe the medication in what is called a depot injection. The person will be given the injection every two to six weeks. The depot slowly releases the medication into the blood stream, making sure there is a steady amount until the next injection is given. Injections are more likely to be given to people who sometimes forget to take tablets.

Why is medication prescribed?

Chemicals carry different messages from brain cell to brain cell. Sometimes if we have too little or too much of one chemical, it can lead to a mental health problem (examples are given in Chapter 2). Medication reverses these problems and restores the right amount of chemicals in the brain.

Side effects

As well as treating the mental health problem medications can also cause unwanted side effects. These side effects are caused because the medication affects other parts of the brain or body as well as the one it is trying to target. For example, a medication that is still sometimes given for schizophrenia is chlorpromazine. Chlorpromazine reduces the build-up of the chemical 'dopamine' that causes psychotic symptoms. But it also affects parts of the brain that help control our movements, so some people might get tremors or shakes as a side effect.

When prescribing medication the doctor will weigh up the benefits of the medication against the possible side effects. The doctor will tell you about these side effects. Sometimes a doctor might prescribe another medication that counteracts the side effects of the original medication. Recent advances in science, however, have introduced newer drugs, which cause fewer unwanted effects for some mental health problems.

It is important that you as a carer are aware of the possible side effects, as people with intellectual disabilities may not be able to recognize them and/or communicate them to other people. If you think the person you care for is suffering from side effects you should report them to the doctor or nurse as soon as possible.

What information should you get from the doctor or nurse?

When a drug is prescribed to the person you care for there is some information that you should know. Doctors and nurses will normally provide you with this information, but they might need to be reminded. You will need to know:

- What it is prescribed for
- Why the doctor thinks it will be helpful for the person
- What the possible side effects are
- What you should do if the side effects occur
- How the medication should be given (i.e. with water etc.)
- At what times it should be given

If you require further information, you could ask if there are any information leaflets available on medication. There are some leaflets that are available especially for people with intellectual disabilities on medication; these can be obtained from the Elfrida Society (contact details given at the end of the chapter).

How will the medication be monitored?

Once a medication is started there should be a procedure to ensure it is monitored and regularly reviewed. Immediately after a new medication is started it would be normal for the doctor or nurse to want to see the person every four to eight weeks. Once the person is settled on the medication it should be reviewed at least every six months. You can help this process by providing information on the following:

- Is the person agreeing to take the medication and do they take it as prescribed?
- Have their views changed about taking the medication?
- Have the signs and symptoms of the mental health problem gone away or reduced?
- Have they had any side effects?
- Do you think it has improved their quality of life?

Biological interventions for depression

A person suffering from depression may be prescribed medication to take. New antidepressant medication has fewer unwanted effects and is safer than older ones. Antidepressants are not addictive. They can be prescribed by a GP. There are two main categories.

(1) SELECTIVE SEROTONIN REUPTAKE INHIBITORS (SSRIS)

Low levels of a certain chemical in the brain called serotonin cause depression. These types of drugs increase the amount of it in the brain. Examples are given in Table 4.1.

Table 4.1 Selective Serotonin Reuptake Inhibitors (SSRIs)

Chemical name	Brand name
citalopram	Cipramil
fluoxetine	Prozac
paroxetine	Seroxat
fluvoxamine	Faverin
sertraline	Lustral

The most common side effects of these drugs are nausea and headaches, although they may also cause restlessness, irritability, anxiety and some difficulty in getting off to sleep. These side effects are generally mild and usually only occur in the first few days of taking the medication. When coming off these tablets, it is important not to stop them suddenly, but to tail off the dose gradually with the advice of a doctor.

(2) TRICYCLIC ANTIDEPRESSANTS

These types of drugs interfere with two brain chemicals: serotonin and noradrenaline. This group includes the examples given in Table 4.2.

Table 4.2 Tricyclic antidepressants

Chemical name	Brand name
amitriptyline	Lentizol, Tryptizol
clomipramine	Anafranil
dothiepin	Prothiaden
lofepramine	Gamanil
imipramine	Tofranil

These drugs are more sedative than the SSRIs, and can cause more trouble-some side effects, such as a dry mouth, blurred vision, dizziness, constipation and difficulty passing water, which can rule out their use in the elderly. However, they are effective antidepressants and suit some people well. If taken as an overdose these drugs can cause heart irregularities.

Most people with an episode of depression respond to the first drug they try. For all antidepressants it takes about 3 to 4 weeks before any change in mood is apparent. The improvement in mood is gradual, and a person may still have 'bad days' even though they are significantly better. It is important that the drug is tried for at least one month, and is taken regularly as prescribed.

Some depressed people require higher doses of the drug than is first prescribed. The doctor will gradually increase the dose, which usually results in the expected improvement in mood. If this does not happen, or if side effects are intolerable, the doctor will probably prescribe from a different group of antidepressants. Also, the doctor might do a blood test to check whether the drug is at the correct levels in the bloodstream for it to work effectively.

If a depressed person is experiencing delusions or hallucinations, the doctor may prescribe some antipsychotic medication such as chlorpromazine (Largactil), haloperidol (Serenace), olanzapine (Zyprexa) or risperidone (Risperdal). One of these drugs may also be used in a low dose if the person is experiencing anxiety or irritability.

Circumstances such as profoundly low mood and failure to eat or drink are life threatening. Overwhelming suicidal thoughts may mean a person needs 24-hour nursing care and more intensive treatment. Admission to a specialized mental health unit may be needed to provide appropriate assessment and treatment.

Biological interventions for manic depression: mood-stabilizing medicines

Manic depression is treated with mood-stabilizing medicines such as lithium.

LITHIUM (BRAND NAMES INCLUDE CAMCOLT, LISKONUM, PRIADEL)

People with manic depression get depressed and need antidepressants to lift their mood, but they may suddenly swing the other way to become manic, needing sedation. To prevent these huge swings in mood, which are so disruptive, a person is prescribed lithium. Although slight changes of mood may still occur, the lithium should reduce the 'highs' and 'lows'. Lithium is sometimes also prescribed to help manage people with challenging behaviour.

Lithium is taken on a long-term basis to prevent relapses. It is an effective medicine but can have serious side effects. Before starting lithium the doctor will ask for blood tests to check kidney and thyroid function. Once the blood level of the drug has been stabilized blood tests are then done at about six-monthly intervals.

Side effects include nausea, loose bowels, tiredness, hand tremor, feeling thirsty and passing a lot of urine. These may improve after a while. Chronic side effects include tremor, weight gain, drinking a lot, passing a lot of urine, and slight forgetfulness. Some people on lithium become hypothyroid (that is, their thyroid gland is under-active) and need to be treated with thyroxine. If the person shows appetite loss, vomiting, diarrhoea, hand trembling, slurred speech, unsteadiness on his or her feet or sleepiness a doctor must be contacted immediately.

Also, it is important to know that, if the person is prescribed lithium, they *must* stay on the same brand.

CARBAMAZEPINE (BRAND NAME: TEGRETOL)

Carbamazepine is normally given for epilepsy but it can also be used to stabilize mood disorders. Although lithium is thought to be more effective, carbamazepine has the advantage of having fewer side effects. Sometimes if lithium is not effective at controlling mood fluctuations then carbamazepine is added. It is also sometimes used in the control of challenging behaviour and epilepsy.

A common side effect is a generalized rash. This is not dangerous and goes away when the medicine is stopped. Some people get nausea and vomiting. Although rare, it is important for you to look out for signs of dizziness, drowsiness, double vision, persistent fever, sore throat, bruising or bleeding. If these occur consult a doctor immediately.

Biological interventions for schizophrenia

Schizophrenia is a type of psychotic disorder. A person with a psychotic disorder loses some contact with reality. When this happens antipsychotic medication (also known as neuroleptics) can be prescribed to help. Antipsychotic medication can reduce or alleviate symptoms (voices, irrational beliefs and delusions) in up to 70 per cent of people who suffer from a psychotic illness (schizophrenia, manic depression). Unlike tranquillizers, antipsychotics are not addictive – that is, people do not develop a craving for them. They differ in their sedative and antipsychotic properties and side effects.

In recent years newer antipsychotics have come on the market such as risperidone and olanzapine. These tend to produce fewer side effects than older drugs.

Clozapine (brand name: Clozaril) is used for people with treat-ment-resistant schizophrenia. It requires a monthly blood test to monitor the functioning of the immune system (white blood cells). Otherwise the person may become vulnerable to infection.

Other antipsychotics include haloperidol (brand name: Serenace), chlorpromazine (brand name: Largactil) and trifluoperazine (brand name: Stelazine).

SIDE EFFECTS

Unfortunately, antipsychotics may have some unwanted side effects which must be weighed against their benefits. Sometimes, soon after someone starts the medicine, the person may develop a tremor of their fingers, dribble saliva and find it difficult to move because they feel rigid. These symptoms are similar to those experienced by people who have Parkin-son's disease and so they are called parkinsonian symptoms. Drugs such as procyclidine (brand name: Kemadrin) or orphenadrine (brand name: Disipal) may be given to treat these. The side effects may decline with time or if the dose of antipsychotics is reduced. It is therefore important to review medication regularly. Also the person may become restless and fidgety. This restlessness especially affects the legs and has been described as an inability to sit still.

Some of these medicines can lower blood pressure. People will complain of feeling dizzy when they get up from their bed or chair, and may fall and hurt themselves. The elderly are particularly vulnerable. It is important for those who experience dizziness to take care. Fortunately, the dizziness usually disappears after the person has been on the medicine for a few weeks.

Abnormal face and body movements may occur. People may clench their jaw, stick out their tongue or, rarely, have a severe reaction where their body is rigidly bent backwards, their head is bent backwards, their eyes are rolled upwards and their tongue is stuck out. In that case, the person will have to go to casualty and may require an injection of procyclidine.

People who are treated with these medicines can put on weight because the medicines increase appetite. Some antipsychotics make the skin sensitive to the sun, so sunscreen must be applied before going out in the sun. Many people with intellectual disabilities suffer with epilepsy; antipsychotic medication may interfere with the control of this, so anti-epileptic medication may need to be reviewed.

Antipsychotics should be taken at the lowest effective dose. Some people with schizophrenia need to be on them continuously. Sometimes it is better to give someone the medicine in the form of a depot injection, as described in the section above. Anxiolytics are also used in the short term (see below).

Biological interventions for anxiety

For mild anxiety psychological interventions such as psychotherapy or relaxation training are usually the best.

Anxiolytics are medicines for reducing anxiety. These include beta-blockers and benzodiazepines. Beta-blockers can be used to help treat the biological symptoms of anxiety, e.g. palpitations, sweating, shakiness etc. They are usually used to help heart conditions such as hypertension (high blood pressure), angina, etc. Some examples are given in Table 4.3.

Table 4.3 Beta-blockers

Chemical name	Brand name
Atenolol	Tenormin
Oxprenolol	Trasicor, Slow-Trasicor, Apsolox
Propranolol	Inderal, Inderal-LA

HOW DO BETA-BLOCKERS WORK FOR ANXIETY?

When we are anxious, our brain becomes more active and alert. Our brain may then make more of the chemicals called noradrenaline and adrenaline. These will then cause our body to have a faster heart rate, shake, sweat etc. and make us feel more anxious. Beta-blockers reduce the effect of these chemicals and so reduce these symptoms of anxiety.

Beta-blockers should start to work on the symptoms fairly soon after taking them, e.g. within a few hours. After that the doctor may need to change the dose to suit the person. The beta-blockers are best taken in a fairly low dose as a 'first aid' measure. They are not addictive. They only act on the physical symptoms and not the cause of anxiety. It is not a good idea to stop taking a beta-blocker suddenly if it has been used every day for more than 4 to 6 weeks, although there probably would be no great problem. A gradual reduction in the dose is probably best.

If the person forgets to take a dose they should start again as soon as they remember unless it is almost time for the next dose. Never try to catch up by taking two or more doses at once as this might cause more side effects. If several doses are missed they should start again when they remember. Tell the doctor about this at the next appointment.

Common side effects include fatigue and the person's toes and fingers might feel cold. These may happen early on in treatment and should go away. If the person feels like this for more than a week after starting the beta-blocker, the doctor should be told. It may be possible to adjust the dose slightly.

Uncommon side effects include stomach upset, sleep problems (not being able to sleep very well and maybe having nightmares) and dizziness. The doctor should be told about these at the next appointment. If the person gets dry eyes the doctor should be contacted as soon as possible. If the person is wheezy or has a slow pulse or skin trouble the doctor should be contacted immediately.

Some people feel a little drowsy, particularly when they first start taking beta-blockers, but this should wear off. If they do feel drowsy, they should not drive or operate machinery. It is against the law to drive or attempt to drive when unfit because of drugs.

Do not be worried by this list of side effects. It is possible that the person who uses these medicines gets none of these side effects as they are rare. On the other hand if the person develops any unusual symptoms they should ask the doctor about them. Be aware that alcohol may slightly reduce the effect of the beta-blocker, but this is unlikely to be a problem.

The doctor should know about any other medicines the person is taking. Also the doctor should know about any heart, breathing, thyroid or diabetic problems in the past (e.g. you should not normally take a beta-blocker if you have asthma). The doctor should know before starting or stopping these or any other drugs. There is no need for a blood test to check on the beta-blocker, although the doctor may want to check the person's blood for other reasons.

BENZODIAZEPINES

A doctor may prescribe benzodiazepines for the short-term where anxiety is complicated by other mental health problems or physical illness. Also they can be used for the control of intensely disturbed behaviour, as they are rapidly sedative when given by injection. Many carers of people with epilepsy will know that medicines like clonazepam (Rivotril) are used to control epilepsy. They can also help in the withdrawal from other drugs, such as alcohol. They should be limited to the lowest possible dose for the shortest possible time (e.g. diazepam, one of the benzodiazepines, is also a hypnotic drug because it is used to induce sleep – see also Chapter 8).

A common side effect is that benzodiazepines are addictive. After about a week, the same dose no longer has the desired effect and more has to be taken to get the same effect. Taking too much of a benzodiazepine may cause intoxication; the person may become unsteady, drowsy and may slur their speech. Stopping the medicine can make the person feel even more anxious, restless, unable to sleep, sweaty, confused, prone to head-aches, and craving for the medicine. Weaning an addicted person from hypnotic drugs like the benzodiazepines can be a slow, difficult process.

BUSPIRONE (BRAND NAME: BUSPAR)

This is used for short-term treatment of anxiety. It may help someone be able to use psychological treatments, and once these are established can be stopped.

ANTIDEPRESSANTS

Some antidepressants (see section on 'Biological interventions for depression' earlier in this chapter) are used in the treatment of anxiety and related disorders.

Biological interventions for dementia

In dementia there is progressive loss of brain cells. This process is currently irreversible. However, there are medicines that can slow the process. Vitamin E, Hormone Replacement Therapy (HRT), non-steroid anti-inflammatory medication and a low dose of aspirin may all help to slow down dementia. Cholinesterase inhibitors (brand names: Aricept, Exelon and Reminyl) are a group of drugs that are used currently in the general population. It is also advised that being more mentally active can be a protective mechanism.

Psychological interventions

Psychological interventions help people to deal with their feelings. They help people with mental, emotional and behavioural problems. Often when someone talks about being 'in therapy' or 'having psychotherapy', these are the types of therapies that they mean. There are many different types of psychological interventions. You might wish to know more about what is on offer, what the psychological approaches to mental health problems are and what each entails.

Some therapies are commonly available through the NHS and some others might be available through the private and voluntary sectors. Referrals are accepted from GPs or mental health professionals. The start of the process involves a meeting between the person and the therapist. Together they decide on the suitability of the therapy to the person's needs and some specific goals for how to change.

If you are choosing a therapist privately you need to check that the therapist is registered with a recognized accreditation body such as the UK Council for Psychotherapists (UKCP) or the British Confederation of Psychotherapists (BCP). Similarly, Chartered Psychologists are registered under the British Psychological Society (BPS) which is a statutory body.

Psychological interventions include the following:

- Cognitive behavioural therapy (CBT)
- Psychodynamic psychotherapy
- Counselling

- Behaviour therapy and skills training methods
- Family therapy
- Therapy sessions in groups
- Other therapies
  - Dramatherapy
  - Art therapy
  - Music therapy

Cognitive behavioural therapy (CBT)

Cognitive behavioural therapy (also known as CBT) is based on the idea that a person's beliefs about what they do, and their reasons for doing them, are as important as what they actually do. In other words a person's thinking, assumptions and beliefs about the world are as important as his or her actions. The main aim of this type of therapy is to change the way the person thinks about certain situations, which in turn could help him or her to cope better. For example, depressed people tend to think that they are not good at anything. This thought would affect the way they view a successful event (e.g. 'it was pure luck') and how they cope with failure (e.g. self-blame: 'I always fail'). In cognitive behavioural therapy the person will learn not to generalize these negative thoughts over all aspects of life (e.g. 'I have been unsuccessful in one area').

WHAT HAPPENS IN COGNITIVE BEHAVIOURAL THERAPY?

During the sessions the therapist will help the person to identify negative or irrational thoughts or thinking patterns (cognitive) and unhelpful patterns of acting (behavioural). For example the irrational fears of a person who suffers from agoraphobia (fear of open spaces) might cause them to stay at home all the time (unwanted behaviour), which can have tremendous consequences on the person's quality of life.

The therapeutic process depends on the collaboration between the therapist and the client. This is done during individual therapy sessions and then practised at home. Usually it lasts for between 6 and 20 individual sessions.

WHO IS COGNITIVE BEHAVIOURAL THERAPY FOR?

This kind of therapy has helped many people with mild to moderate depression, anxiety, obsessive compulsive disorders, bulimia, phobias and panic disorders. It is also used in schizophrenia, as most people still experience psychotic symptoms (e.g. voices), though less frequently and intensely when they are on medication. It is clear that the person must be motivated and able to communicate the content of their thoughts to the therapist, though this may need to include the use of non-verbal materials such as drawings and symbols.

Psychodynamic psychotherapy

The theory behind this approach has been around for a long time. It has been adapted for those with intellectual disabilities and mental health problems over the last 20 years. It involves talking to a qualified psychodynamic psychotherapist who in turn will help the person to understand their feelings.

WHAT HAPPENS IN PSYCHODYNAMIC PSYCHOTHERAPY?

The psychotherapist adopts a listening stance and allows the person to talk about what they want. The focus is on the person's conscious and unconscious assumptions about relationships and how these are played out with the therapist during the therapy session. Thus past experiences resurface and can be thought about in a live way. The therapist avoids imposing his or her view and the person in turn is asked to live with the uncertainty aroused by this.

WHO IS PSYCHODYNAMIC PSYCHOTHERAPY FOR?

People with anxiety or relationship problems might benefit from psychodynamic psychotherapy. To undergo therapy they must be able to tolerate anxiety during the therapeutic process and not act out their anxiety by resorting to behaviours such as self-harming or alcohol abuse.

Counselling

The counsellor tries to help the person to overcome emotional problems through a combination of talking and listening.

WHAT HAPPENS IN COUNSELLING?

Listening to the person talking is important because the main purpose is to help the client understand him or herself more clearly. By thinking aloud the person can become aware of links between aspects of feelings and behaviour that previously have been unrecognized. The counsellor explains the rationale and that has the effect of making problems more understandable and therefore gives the person the confidence that he or she can solve the problems. The development of trust between the therapist and the person is important. It allows communication in words, and it promotes the understanding and integration of previously unacknowledged aspects of the self and relationships.

Behavioural therapy

Behavioural therapy suggests that apparent behaviour has been learnt. Behavioural therapy aims to identify and directly change unwanted behaviours. Or, alternatively, unwanted behaviours are ignored whilst more positive socially valued behaviours are rewarded. Less attention is paid to what has actually caused these unwanted behaviours.

WHO IS BEHAVIOURAL THERAPY FOR?

This kind of therapy can be used with people who have limited or no verbal communication skills, although the ability to communicate one's thoughts and feelings can give valuable information for behaviour therapy. Again in order to reach a successful result the person has to co-operate as much as possible with the intervention plan.

WHAT HAPPENS IN BEHAVIOURAL THERAPY?

Current behaviour management combines the teaching of new skills together with the suppression of undesirable behaviours. There are several ways of encouraging and increasing new behaviours. Some carers might have used these techniques at home over the years without even realizing. These techniques are widely used and include the following:

- The ABC approach
- Positive reinforcement
- Prompting
- Shaping
- Chaining
- Relaxation training
- Role-playing
- Modelling
- Desensitization

Some items on the list are briefly explained below, as they are particularly relevant to people with intellectual disabilities and mental health problems. Carers might be asked to help the person they care for to use some of these at home.

The ABC approach

In traditional behaviour management, the problem is studied and then the environment is manipulated in such a way as to increase, decrease or maintain the behaviour. This is known as the ABC approach. The problem or, as it is otherwise called, the target *Behaviour* is described and then either the *Antecedents* and/or the *Consequences* of that behaviour are manoeuvred. This is described in more detail in Chapter 5 on challenging behaviour.

Relaxation training

In recent years research evidence has shown that the use of relaxation techniques in people with intellectual disabilities and behavioural problems is beneficial. Behavioural relaxation training involves the demonstration of 'tense' and then 'relaxed' states in different body areas. During the session the therapist demonstrates first and the person just observes. Later the therapist provides prompting and feedback according to performance. It includes the following steps:

- Sitting in a relaxed posture
- Tension release cycles in the hands and face
- Breathing slowly and deeply

The person is asked to repeat the tension release cycles in different parts of the body. Alternative methods of relaxation include deep breathing exercises and listening to soothing music. Once the person has mastered these techniques it is hoped that they will use them in everyday life situations that they find difficult in order to counteract anger or anxiety and become relaxed and calm. Audiotaped instructions or soothing music may help self-initiated relaxation.

People who have intellectual disabilities may experience a number of fears and anxieties in everyday life. The process of relocation from hospital to a community setting might cause anxiety for example, or the presence of behavioural difficulties might hinder the relocation process itself. Relaxation training might be part of a treatment plan aimed to make these difficulties easier to cope with.

Family therapy

Most people with intellectual disabilities live with their families or in 'family' groups such as group homes where they are supported by staff teams. Working with the person and their family can boost the therapeutic process.

WHAT HAPPENS IN FAMILY THERAPY?

Families often want to be involved and can benefit individually and collectively from the experience. Issues such as loss, isolation, ambivalence, anxieties about sexuality and concerns about failure can be explored with the family members helping each other. The roles of various family members including the individual themselves can be helpfully explored, particularly where the individual has been assigned a role of being 'special'. The person with intellectual disabilities may be helping to keep a family or parental relationship together or may be the focus of expression of parental relationship difficulties. Siblings may also find themselves trying to fulfil a role of being special or particularly successful.

Staff or carer groups form part of a complex and dynamic system around an individual. The interactions of this system together with its environment can be significant in terms of predisposing, precipitating or maintaining factors that contribute to behaviour or mental health problems.

Therapy sessions in groups

Group therapy might be preferable for someone who finds the idea of one-to-one therapy too intense and for certain mental health problems.

WHAT HAPPENS IN GROUP THERAPY?

In this, although the therapist plays an important role, other group members are also of vital importance in helping people to assess their experience. There is a feeling of belonging that develops while group members meet regularly at the same place to discuss issues.

WHO IS GROUP THERAPY FOR?

Group therapy might be appropriate for people who have benefited from individual therapy and still have difficulties in relationships. Such groups might also help with anger management, anxiety management, and social skills. In the field of intellectual disabilities there has been an ongoing debate as to whether these individuals can benefit from the therapy.

People who undergo therapy learn to be in touch with their feelings and that can be a difficult thing to face up to for anyone. Intellectual disabilities do not prevent someone from having a rich emotional life. Therefore people with mild or moderate intellectual disabilities can benefit from counselling or psychoanalysis as long as they understand the purpose of the treatment and are motivated.

Some people have 'concrete thinking' which means that they cannot link their thoughts and actions to their feelings so might not benefit from psychotherapy. People with severe intellectual disabilities may not be suitable for talking therapies (although they might have a rich emotional life) because of their extremely limited intellectual abilities often coupled with limited verbal skills. Some therapists have used alternative ways of communicating such as with symbols.

Other therapies

Other therapies include:

- Art therapy
- Dramatherapy
- Music therapy

ART THERAPY

This can be used in individual and group settings. People use whatever art processes are most comfortable for them. The emphasis is on the person's unconscious processes that are expressed in symbols through their artwork. People are actively involved in their own therapy. Their method of communication is respected and enhanced, supporting feelings of self-worth and confidence which can enable the person to become more creative and independent in their lives.

Art therapy can make an important contribution to people who exhibit autistic characteristics.

DRAMATHERAPY

This is the intentional and systematic use of drama/theatre processes to achieve psychological growth and change. The tools are derived from theatre and the goals are psychotherapeutic.

In other words, dramatherapy is involvement in drama with a healing intention. Dramatherapy facilitates change through drama processes. It uses the potential of drama to reflect and transform life experiences to enable people to express and work through problems they are encountering or to maintain a person's well-being and health.

A connection is created between the person's inner world, problematic situation or life experience and the activity in the dramatherapy session. Activities seek to achieve awareness of self and other.

What happens in dramatherapy?

The dramatherapist works with groups or individuals over a number of weeks for sessions lasting between forty minutes and one and a half hours. Each session usually consists of a 'warm up' phase, which develops into an 'active exploration' of areas that are problematic for the people taking part, followed by a 'closure'. The kind of problems which can be dealt with and the form of the sessions are extremely varied. Dramatherapy takes place within clear boundaries, which protect the therapeutic space. Dramatherapists use a variety of media such as puppets, music, movement and dance, interactive games, story telling and enactment.

Who is dramatherapy for?

Dramatherapy is practised with groups and individuals across the full range of ability, and in care settings such as clinics, hospitals and specialist centres such as adolescent units. It is also offered as an individual or group therapy available outside institutions. In the case of profound and multiple disabilities the focus is on building a one-to-one relationship through play and sensory activities.

MUSIC THERAPY

Music therapy in Britain has been used within the field of intellectual disabilities for many years. The therapist helps the person to achieve change, using musical experiences and the relationships that develop through them.

What happens in music therapy?

Sessions normally take place weekly over a period of time and, in common with other therapies, consistency and trust is important. Although the emphasis is on playing or listening to live music as a means of developing the relationship, it is not necessary for the person to have any musical training or apparent ability.

The music therapist will provide a selection from a wide range of instruments. People are offered the opportunity to play any of these, or choose to vocalize, move around or simply sit and listen. The therapist pays attention to the quality of the person's music or actions and responds with improvised music. This can support, contain and challenge in a similar way to spoken language but it also reaches and engages people at a different level.

Who is music therapy for?

This is of benefit for those for whom words are not readily accessible but is also valuable to others. The use of improvised music brings unconscious areas into awareness. Music therapy has been used at all developmental stages and with people with autism. It allows for choice and the growth of self-esteem and the fostering of an awareness of self and other.

Social interventions

A social intervention is something that is done to help the person by changing an aspect of their environment or social circumstances.

As part of the assessment process clinicians will try to find out what factors or events contributed to the development of the mental health problem. These factors might be of a social nature, i.e. at school, family, at work or a day centre. When they have been identified, it may be possible to intervene and manipulate them by changing the environment or the situation. In other words a social intervention might be useful.

When a person finds him or herself in a situation that doesn't meet their needs or wants (e.g. unemployment, homelessness, low level of stimulation and scarcity of attention, not being given the opportunity to make own decisions) they can be affected by environmental factors. For example, a person may develop an anxiety disorder if their job requirements change and the person is stretched beyond their resources. By adapting the job requirements to match their skills, the person's anxiety disorder might settle. If the anxiety disorder persists then more changes to environmental factors may be needed. Or it might be that a combination of psychological and biological (medication) interventions is needed as well.

Social interventions can address areas such as housing, financial assistance, education, social activities, family and peer relationships and mixing with others, leisure and so on.

Helping the person to communicate

Very often people with intellectual disabilities have problems in communicating with other people. Estimates suggest that 50 per cent to 90 per cent of people with intellectual disabilities have communication difficulties. About 60 per cent of people with intellectual disabilities have some skills in symbolic communication using pictures, signs or symbols. About 20 per cent have no verbal communication skills but do demonstrate a will to communicate, expecting a response.

People with intellectual disabilities are often dependent on professional intervention to develop a communication plan that is best for them. Assessment can work out the most effective means of communication for each individual across all environments, with speech and language therapists being key professionals.

Communication between individuals or groups of people is very important in everyday life. It is the key to our existence and it is how we learn. By communicating we can tell other people our feelings, thoughts and emotions, and it allows us to be included in society. In everyday life people usually communicate with others by speaking or writing. If someone cannot speak, understand words, read or write then they often feel like they are not allowed to be part of everyday activities. They might feel that they are excluded from things, and feel undervalued or not appreciated by other people.

Different ways of communicating, however, should be equally valued and accepted. People with intellectual disabilities can be misunderstood and excluded since they may need different ways of communicating which require all the people around them to learn their language (e.g. sign language; Makaton and Signalong). Not being able to communicate effectively with others leads to frustration. Frustration can lead to withdrawal or anger and aggression expressed against self or others. This is seen as challenging behaviour. Challenging behaviour can result in exclusion from school, from college, from employment, or from all social activities. A high percentage of communication, however, is non-verbal. Objects, pictures, signs and symbols are all powerful ways of conveying meaning such as the British Sign Language used by deaf people and Braille, which is used by blind people to read. Today, technology provides ever more effective ways of accessing graphics and communication aids.

People with more severe and complex needs may not be able to use any of the recognized means of communicating and will be dependent on others to interpret their needs and choices.

In recent years approaches such as Phoebe Caldwell's learning through play, Individualized Sensory Environments, Intensive Interaction (Nind and Hewett 2001), as well as the technological development of Multi-Sensory Rooms, have increased our knowledge and awareness of non-verbal behaviour so that we can respond to and encourage individuals with respect at whatever stage they have reached in their communication development. You can get more information about these from the British Institute of Learning Disabilities (BILD) (contact details given at the end of this chapter).

Carers' support with interventions

Therapeutic interventions are part of the person's treatment or care plan and therefore are part of his or her daily life or routine. Your support with interventions can be very helpful. For example, you might be asked to help the person you are caring for to repeat at home some of the techniques or skills that have been taught by the therapist or the clinician. Carers often act as advocates as well, by helping individuals to make important decisions about treatment plans.

Resources

British Institute of Learning Disabilities (BILD)

Campion House
Green Street
Kidderminster
Worcestershire DY10 1JL
Tel: 01562 723010
Fax: 01562 723029
Website: www.bild.org.uk
Email: enquiries@bild.org.uk

(Information, fact sheets, publications and training)

The Elfrida Society
The Tom Blyth Centre
34 Islington Park Street
London N1 1PX
Tel: 020 7359 7443
Fax: 020 7704 1354
Website: www.elfrida.com
Email: elfrida@elfrida.com

(Information leaflets for people with intellectual disabilities about medication)

Chapter 5

Challenging Behaviour

Theresa Joyce, Mary Jane Spiller and Anastasia Gratsa

Key messages from this chapter
What is challenging behaviour?
How common is challenging behaviour?
Explanations of a difficult or challenging behaviour
Functional analysis of challenging behaviour
Components of a functional analysis and assessment process
Different kinds of therapeutic interventions
Monitoring of interventions
Consent

Key messages from this chapter

- Challenging behaviour is not an illness, but is a form of socially inappropriate or unacceptable behaviour that can develop for a number of different reasons. For example, it can be something a person learns to do in order to let other people know what they want, or what they are feeling. It can also develop as a result of a mental or physical illness, or as a result of abuse.

- It is usually thought that challenging behaviour has a 'function' or purpose. In other words, the challenging behaviour might be

---

continued…

...continued

used by the person as a way to communicate something to others around them.

- 'Functional analysis' is a means of developing an understanding of the function of a challenging behaviour for an individual. It consists of gathering information, in a structured way, to work out what makes the behaviour useful for the person.

- Therapeutic interventions are based on adequate understanding of the behaviour, are individually tailored and aim to replace the challenging behaviour with a more appropriate one. Removing the behaviour will not remove the purpose that it served for the individual.

- The aim is to replace dysfunctional behaviours with more functional ones, in order to ensure that the person is not restricted in their access to the community and an improved quality of life.

- Professionals must also obtain the person's informed consent or involve a responsible carer or advocate. Professionals must

What is challenging behaviour?

Challenging behaviour is behaviour that people think is abnormal or unusual within the person's culture. Examples could include:

- Someone being aggressive to themselves or to others

- Someone damaging property

- Someone screaming and other socially inappropriate behaviours

- Someone refusing to take part in activities and other more 'resistant' types of behaviours

This type of behaviour is seen as a problem because of what it can do to the person involved and others around them. These behaviours can physically hurt people. They can also stop people from doing what they want. It might make their life more difficult because they find it hard to get along with other people in their community.

This makes it a challenge for services (such as health or social services) to support this person. For people with challenging behaviour who live with their families or other carers, then the challenge is also in providing support for them.

To respond to this challenge the focus of the problem needs to be shifted away from the person involved. Services also need to be developed to meet their individual needs appropriately. Challenging behaviour is often learnt. Sometimes it results from an underlying physical or mental health problem.

How common is challenging behaviour?

Studies in the UK have suggested that approximately 6 per cent of people who have intellectual disabilities probably have challenging behaviour. Some evidence suggests that challenging behaviours can start in childhood and persist into adulthood.

Challenging behaviours appear to be more common amongst men. Some challenging behaviours seem to be related to additional physical or sensory disability, such as difficulties in getting around or problems with hearing or seeing. Some types of challenging behaviour such as self-injury also appear to be related to communication difficulties.

Explanations of a difficult or challenging behaviour

Most people believe that a lot of challenging behaviour is something a person has learnt to do because of the way people around them have reacted to their actions. For example someone might deliberately hurt himself or herself because they have learnt that when they do this, their carers stop asking them to take part in an activity that they do not want to do. Alternatively, someone might learn that if they scream or shout, their carer usually gives them a drink. This is in order to stop them screaming.

It is therefore thought that challenging behaviour has a 'function'; or in other words it has a purpose or meaning for the person involved. Disruptive behaviours like aggression and self-injury could have many different functions, such as:

- Showing a need for help or attention
- Escaping from stressful situations or activities

- Getting an object that they want

- Protesting against unwanted events/activities

- Getting stimulation

Something called a **functional assessment** is used to work out what the function of a challenging behaviour is. From doing this a substitute or alternative behaviour can then be taught to help the person get his or her message across in a more appropriate way.

The person probably did not start to behave like this in order to get a reward, but instead the behaviour happened and was for some reason reinforced. In other words another person reacted to the behaviour in such a way that it helped to reinforce it, to make the person want to do it again in order to get the same reaction. This reaction is called a 'reinforcer': a consequence that strengthens behaviour. (See Figures 5.1 and 5.2.)

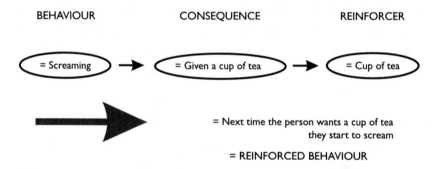

Figure 5.1 Example of a reinforced behaviour 1

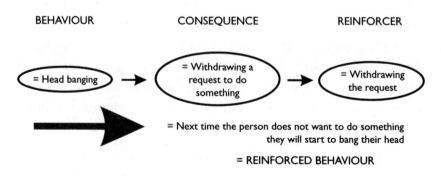

Figure 5.2 Example of a reinforced behaviour 2

A reinforcer is individually determined – not everyone likes the same thing. Also a reinforcer may be very powerful at one time, and not at another. For example, a slice of cake may be very reinforcing if you have been starved of sweet things for a week, but might not be if you have just eaten nearly a whole cake.

Often, explanations for challenging behaviour given by carers will be things like frustration, anger or sadness. For example, 'Jon is screaming because he is frustrated.' The problem with this type of explanation is that it is not really useful for planning an intervention or a treatment plan. Psychologists try to understand the **function** or **purpose** of the behaviour and what the person is trying to say. In order to understand challenging behaviour they have developed a type of assessment called the **Antecedent Behaviour Consequences (ABC)** approach (see Figure 5.3). This involves identifying the 'antecedents' or triggers to the behaviour and also describing what happens as a result of the behaviour – the consequences.

- **Antecedent:** asked to do the washing up
- **Behaviour:** head-banging and screaming
- **Consequences:** request withdrawn

Other important areas looked at include **individual** and **environmental factors**, and the person's ability to communicate. The **context** that the behaviour occurs in can also be important. This can include the emotional state of the person or the environment in which they find themselves. For

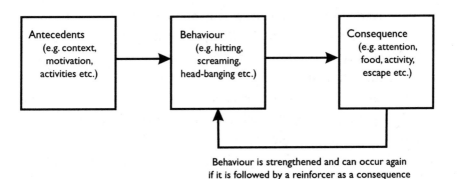

Behaviour is strengthened and can occur again
if it is followed by a reinforcer as a consequence

Figure 5.3 The ABC approach

example a person may only be aggressive when they get to the day centre if they have had to sit on a bus with someone making a noise for a long time. This noise has made them feel irritated or stressed, and so when someone at the day centre asks them to do something they refuse. Or they may only show challenging behaviour in certain places or with certain people – these can act as **triggers** to indicate that a reinforcer is likely (or unlikely) to occur.

This model of challenging behaviour has mainly been developed for people with more severe intellectual disabilities, although it can also be used with people who have less severe disabilities.

There are other possible causes. Challenging behaviour may be a symptom of a mental health problem. It is difficult to diagnose a mental health problem in someone with severe intellectual disabilities, as they probably cannot describe their symptoms. It is usually less difficult where the individual has mild intellectual disabilities and is able to report on them. If there is a mental health problem, then this will need treatment, as well as making sure a functional assessment is done.

Challenging behaviour may also be the result of abuse or trauma. The rate of sexual abuse amongst people with intellectual disabilities is much higher than for the general population and many individuals may not be able to indicate their distress in words and so display challenging behaviour instead.

It may also be as a result of a physical illness or pain. It is important to make sure that there is no physical illness, especially if the challenging behaviour started suddenly. This is an important part of the assessment process. For example, an individual may become aggressive when approached by someone, but the reason may be that they are in pain and want to avoid being touched.

It may also be as a result of chemical interactions in the brain. One example is the possibility that self-injury is maintained by the release of B-endorphins ('happy chemicals') in the brain, which act as a reinforcer by altering the person's mood and making them feel happier. The causes of challenging behaviour are summarized in Figure 5.4.

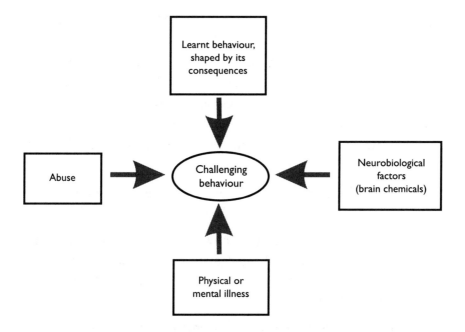

Figure 5.4 Causes of challenging behaviour

Functional analysis of challenging behaviour

Although the behaviour itself may be inappropriate, the need that it is meeting is not. **Functional analysis** is a type of assessment that is done to work out the function of the behaviour for the person involved. By doing a functional analysis of the challenging behaviour psychologists can work out the best way to teach someone a more appropriate way of letting people know what they want. The aim is not to get rid of the behaviour, but to replace it with more acceptable and appropriate ones. This is more likely to be successful when it is based on the findings of a functional analysis.

Components of a functional analysis and assessment process

The person referred to have a functional analysis will probably have more than one challenging behaviour. Each of these must be considered. The person you care for will be interviewed if possible as well as you and any other carers. The psychologist might also want to spend some time with the person directly observing their behaviour. They would not want to interact with them, or to change what the person is doing, but would want to see what happens for the person normally. This can seem quite strange, especially if the observations are carried out in your home.

The professional who carries out the assessment will need information on the following:

- A detailed history of the development and course of the behaviours

- Detailed information about how often they happen, how long they last for, how bad any damage is, where and when they happen, and what effect they have on the person or those around them

- Detailed information about the environment, including activities that the person takes part in, their daily routine, their friends and social activities, the extent to which the environment supports activities, and the skills of the staff/carers. Enriching the environment in terms of activities and interaction can reduce some challenging behaviours

- Details of what act as reinforcers for the individual

- Detailed information of the person's communication style in case people have overestimated the amount the person can understand

Before the assessment you might be given what are known as 'reactive management strategies'. These can include **de-escalation** and **redirection** strategies (e.g. when a person shouts in anger the carer may ask him or her to engage in an activity in order to divert attention). It is therefore important to understand the build-up to the challenging behaviour, so that you can work out when you need to use these strategies.

It is important to remember that these are not the only interventions you will be given. After the assessment you may be told about other types of interventions to help in the long term.

Information for the assessment might be gathered in a number of different ways. Published assessment guides and checklists of behaviours are often used by the professionals involved. The aim is to discover exactly what the behaviours are – it is not detailed enough to say that the person is aggressive. The behaviour needs to be described in detail (e.g. 'hit John on the shoulder with his fist').

You might also be asked to keep records. There are a number of different types of record keeping, and the type used will mainly depend on how often the behaviour occurs and, to some extent, the severity of the behaviour. Behaviours that happen a lot can be directly observed (usually by a skilled professional, e.g. a psychologist or behavioural support specialist). They can also be recorded using frequency charts, when you might be asked to tick a chart every time the behaviour happens.

ABC charts may also be used. ABC is a way of noting the **antecedents** or triggers to the target behaviour (what was going on before the behaviour occurred), the **behaviour** itself (what the person actually did) and the **consequences** of the behaviour (what the person and others around them did afterwards). You may be asked to note down what happens in three different categories. An example of an ABC chart is presented in Table 5.1.

Table 5.1 Example of an ABC chart

Date	Time	What happened before?	What did he/she do?	What happened afterwards?
11/11/03	12:00	Tony was in a good mood. He was asked to move out of the way or stay and help load the washing machine.	Screamed and was verbally aggressive.	He was ignored.

For each occurrence of challenging behaviour the time and the date must be noted; also details of what happened should be as specific as possible.

The antecedents that need to be considered include the person's mood, build-up to the incident, activities being undertaken and any interaction that was occurring (or not occurring) before the behaviour. The consequences also need to be recorded – for example, whether an activity stopped (or started), how the person was calmed down, or whether they were asked to leave the room etc.

This sort of information is very important to help people understand the function and reasons for the challenging behaviour and for the best intervention to be developed.

Different kinds of therapeutic interventions

The intervention is usually made up of a number of parts, and they are related to the function of the behaviour. They usually focus on what the person finds reinforcing, changing the environment where the challenging behaviour occurs and teaching a more appropriate response than the challenging behaviour.

People with intellectual disabilities often find that the routines of their lives, and the activities they take part in, are determined more by other people than by choosing what they want to do themselves. One aspect of intervention may therefore consist of developing preferred activities – if a person becomes challenging when asked to engage in a particular activity, it may be appropriate to change this for another one which they enjoy and want to participate in.

Challenging behaviour may occur in certain contexts, and changing the environment around the person, or the context in which it occurs, can have significant effects. This may involve making more activities available, changing routines, or changing the way in which an activity is offered. Making these changes is sometimes difficult when there are other family members to be considered, so there should be a lot of discussion between you and the psychologist about what is realistic and useful.

Monitoring of interventions

Interventions must be monitored at regular intervals to make sure they are working (see Figure 5.5). Sometimes minor alterations will be needed to the treatment plan in order to obtain better results. Also, if the unwanted behaviour has worsened, the person with intellectual disabilities will need to be reassessed for new clues and an update on changes (e.g. new workers at the day centre who have replaced those that the person was familiar with, introduction of a new routine or change in medication etc.). Changes in the treatment plan must involve support to staff, carers and family who will be responsible for putting them into practice. It is part of the job of the mental health professional to maintain contact with the people who provide care for the individual, listen to their feedback and involve them in the planning process.

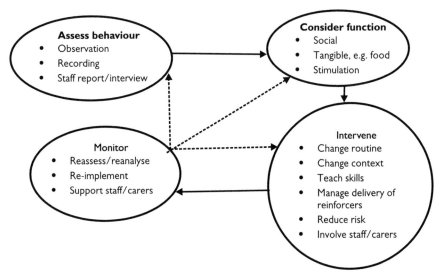

Figure 5.5 The process of assessment and intervention

Consent

It is essential that consent is obtained before the assessment of a person's behavioural difficulties begins. This approval for the process of assessment should extend throughout treatment and into the monitoring stage. If a person is unable to give consent then it is important to consider their best interests with carers and advocates. (See Chapter 6 on law, policy and ethical issues.)

Chapter 6

Law, Policy and Ethical Issues

Anastasia Gratsa

Key messages from this chapter

- Consent is saying yes or no to what happens. Carers or family need to work out if the person can make that decision. It is essential that professionals obtain the person's consent before assessment begins.

- The Mental Health Act (1983) is about to change. Scotland and Northern Ireland have different Mental Health Acts. Under the Mental Health Act (1983) the terms 'mental impairment' and

---

continued...

'severe mental impairment' may be used to describe people
with intellectual disabilities if they present with either abnormally
aggressive behaviour or seriously irresponsible behaviour.
Sections of the Mental Health Act that are relevant to the
provisions for people with mental health problems and
intellectual disabilities are summarized in the Appendix at the
end of the book.

- The Human Rights Act came into force in October 2000. It
follows from the fundamental rights and freedoms found in the
European Convention on Human Rights. It does not create any
new rights, but provides a way for cases to be heard in UK
courts or tribunals that may have had to go to the European
Court of Human Rights before.

- Physical interventions should be used in the context of other
strategies for the person after other less intrusive methods have
been tried and found to be unsuccessful, and as a part of
individual management plans. Such interventions should be
carried out within a legal and ethical framework that sets out
explicit safeguards for the person with intellectual disabilities and
for staff. Staff training and support is essential to ensure good
practice in the use of physical interventions.

Introduction

There are many different issues covered in this chapter that relate to the
law, policy and ethical issues that might concern the person you care for.
Important issues such as confidentiality, capacity to give consent and the
relevant laws are discussed. These issues can be very complicated and confusing, but this chapter gives an overview of the main issues that can
concern an adult with intellectual disabilities and mental health problems.
Contact details of organizations that can provide further details and
support for individual cases are given at the end of the chapter.

Confidentiality

People with intellectual disabilities are more likely to be in situations
where people give their personal information without previously asking

them if it is OK to do so. Carers often find themselves in dilemmas when they need to discuss information with professionals such as doctors or nurses without having the consent of the person with intellectual disabilities. It can be very tricky to know how to resolve this conflict of what or how much information to pass on.

A paid carer explains her difficulty with confidentiality issues during appointments with the psychiatrist:

> If the service user is quite able to speak for themselves you don't feel you can say anything because it's like a power struggle and you feel like you are trying to take away something and you can't say to the service user 'no, you are wrong, you are giving out the wrong information'. It's whether you can contribute without feeling that you are taking over. If you support someone who does not have verbal communication as a member of staff you feel...you are trying to give an impression of what the behaviours are. But if you are supporting someone with verbal communication, who does not want you to be there, and sees the psychiatrist on their own, then you don't get any feedback, so next time you come round you don't know what the issues are for this person because the service user hasn't told you, and you have not been part of that meeting. Psychiatrists, I have to say, do not tell you as a staff team or key workers what is happening. Until you get a report or a complaint letter, six weeks down the line, that is the service user's misrepresentation of the situation or is the situation that happened which needs to be dealt with straight away if it is a protection issue and if it isn't, you still need to know. I have been in situations where I've been in three meetings with no feedback not knowing what is happening.

Confidentiality requires respect for the privacy of other people. Identifiable information to people outside of the situation should only be given with the person's consent or (if they are unable to give or deny consent) in their 'best interests' (see sections 'What can you do?' and 'Capacity to consent').

Some important things to know include the following:

- Confidentiality principles do not include letters to referrers, information shared during team meetings or during supervision
- Professionals should only share information about clients when it helps them to fulfil their professional duties

- An explicit request for information not to be disclosed to particular people must be respected except in exceptional circumstances where the health, safety or welfare of the person or someone else would otherwise be put at serious risk

- If confidentiality is broken without consent, the person should be told what has been said and to whom

If a person expressly opposes contact with the family or carer, mental health professionals often find it difficult to decide when to breach 'patient confidentiality'. Although there is no consensus about the seriousness of the harm that justifies disclosure, a mental health professional would involve the carer against the person's wishes out of concern for the carer's well-being.

What can you do?

You can get an agreement when the person you care for is reasonably well. Agree under which circumstances discussions with you and the mental health team can take place, and what sort of information can be exchanged (e.g. when early warning signs are present).

Discuss disclosure against the person's wishes when it might be in their 'best interests'. The person you care for could be regarded as lacking capacity to make treatment choices. Carer involvement can be seen to be a 'treatment choice'. If the person is lacking capacity you might want to discuss with the mental health team whether maintaining confidentiality is in the person's 'best interests'. Carers can help mental health professionals to think through some possible issues (e.g. nature and seriousness of harm faced by the person and the probability of it occurring). By talking through these issues with the mental health team reasons for breaching or not breaching confidentiality can become clearer to everyone.

Ask the clinician whether he or she might have an additional 'duty of care' towards you. The role of carers as members of the 'care team' in the community presupposes the recognition of the interests of carers. This has been reinforced by one of the standards set by the National Service Framework for Mental Health published in 1999. This framework sets out the standards the Department of Health expects from mental health services. It states that all individuals who provide regular and substantial care for a person on the Care Programme Approach should:

- Have an assessment of their caring, physical and mental health needs, repeated on at least an annual basis

- Have their own written care plan, which is given to them and implemented in discussion with them

It also states that 'the service user's consent should always be explicitly sought before information (about medication, other treatment and care) is passed on to their carer' and that 'if the service user is incapacitated, information may be passed to the carer if it is in the service user's best interests'.

What does it mean to 'give consent'?

Consent is saying yes or no to what happens. Consent is a commonly used word, and can refer to:

- A person giving permission for something

- A person expressing a willingness for something to happen

- A person entering into a voluntary agreement about something

Giving consent *does not* refer to:

- A person going along with something

- A person giving in to something

When someone is asked to give consent to something it is important to make sure that:

- The person is *not* saying yes because they do not feel like they can say no

- The person is *not* saying yes because they are scared of the nurse or doctor and do not feel able to say no to them

- The person is *not* simply choosing the last option given to them, regardless of what it is. If someone is known to do this then the question could be phrased in such a way that gets the desired answer

- The person is *not* saying yes because they always answer yes to any question

- The person is *not* saying no because they always answer no to any question

- The person is aware that they have a choice in accepting or declining an intervention

A person with intellectual disabilities can have problems with communication, and so giving consent is an important area where they may need support. For example, when considering a therapeutic intervention such as medication or psychological therapies, the person may need support to fully understand:

- What the intervention is trying to do

- What the intervention will involve

- The many advantages and disadvantages of the intervention

The person may need extra explanations, more time to make a decision, or to have any written or spoken information given to them in a way that they understand, for example with the use of pictures or signs. This will vary from person to person. Also, the same person may need different levels of support for different types of decisions or at different times.

Capacity to consent

Capacity to consent means how able a person is to make a decision. If someone has the capacity to make a decision it means they can make a decision by themselves, although they may need support to do so. Does the person you care for:

- Understand the nature of the treatment being offered including the likely consequences of having or not having that treatment?

- Appreciate that he or she suffers from a problem affecting their mental health requiring treatment or special help?

- Understand the information they now have about their illness and treatment?

The law says every adult has the right to make his or her own decisions. Just because someone needs help or support to make a decision does not mean carers or professionals can decide for him or her. It is important to support people to decide things for themselves as much as possible. Each decision must be treated differently and every time the person needs to make a decision the health worker should work out if the person can make that decision. You can help with this.

Capacity is a legal concept and concerns an individual's ability to understand what is being suggested and what will happen if they do or do not agree. The person needs to be able to understand and remember the information given to them, believe it and balance the risks and benefits to make a choice. The decision does not need to be the one that others would come to. Someone may have the capacity to make simple decisions but not more complex ones. Similarly, capacity can change in a person due to tiredness, pain or drugs, for instance. The person with intellectual disabilities should, if they have capacity, decide what should happen to them and what they do.

No one can give consent on behalf of an adult who is unable to do so themselves. However, health professionals can still treat such a person if the treatment is in their 'best interests'. 'Best interests' do not just refer to medical interests but also include factors such as general well-being and quality of life. Relatives, carers, friends and/or advocates may be best placed to advise on the person's needs and preferences and should be consulted.

Common law imposes a **duty of care** on all professional staff. Staff can be considered negligent if they do not take appropriate action. If staff act under common law without the consent of the person with intellectual disabilities, for example in the use of restraint when it is needed, then it is good practice to consider whether statutory law, for example the Mental Health Act (1983), should be used as a framework to preserve the rights of the person with intellectual disabilities and to maintain professional standards. If statutory law does not apply, it is essential that checks are put in place to ensure that the principle of 'duty of care' is not used to permit poor or even abusive practice. The principle of 'in the best interests' applies. Organizations should have clear codes of practice on these issues. Guidelines exist on certain procedures (e.g. British Institute of Learning Disabilities (BILD) guidelines on physical interventions).

The Mental Health Act (1983)

The majority of people in need of mental health input readily accept help. However, sometimes a person's mental state, behaviour or functioning may cause concern to others although the person is adamant that he or she does not want or need psychiatric help. The Mental Health Act (1983) is the legal framework that is concerned with the care and treatment of those with mental health problems in England and Wales. It is about to change. Scotland and Northern Ireland have different Mental Health Acts.

The sections that are relevant to people with mental health problems and intellectual disabilities include:

- Detention for assessment
- Detention for treatment
- Rights to appeal against detention
- Discharge back to the community
- Consent to treatment
- Living in the community under guardianship

The Human Rights Act (2000)

Until recently the European Convention of Human Rights was not part of the UK law. The Human Rights Act became law in Britain on 2 October 2000. People can now take their case to a UK court or tribunal. Before, people who felt their human rights were being contravened had to go to the European Court of Human Rights in Strasbourg. This was often expensive and slow and the judgements of the European Court could be ignored.

Since the introduction of the Human Rights Act into UK law people who feel that their rights are being ignored have a direct remedy in the UK courts. Furthermore, the judgements of the European Court of Human Rights are binding in national law.

The Act is designed to protect individuals from abuse by state institutions and people working for these institutions. The Human Rights Act will make it easier to challenge abuse of human rights in the future. Some Articles from the European Convention on Human Rights are relevant to people with intellectual disabilities:

Article 1	No one has the right to unlawfully interfere with your possessions
Article 2	The right to access to education; The right to life
Article 3	No torture, inhumane or degrading treatment
Article 4	No slavery or forced labour
Article 5	The right to liberty and personal freedom
Article 6	The right to a fair trial
Article 7	No punishment without law
Article 8	The right to respect for private and family life
Article 9	Freedom of thought and religion
Article 10	Freedom of expression
Article 11	Freedom of assembly (meeting others)
Article 12	The right to marry and have a family
Article 14	Freedom from discrimination
Article 17	No one has the right to destroy or abuse rights

For example, freedom from inhumane, degrading treatment (Article 3) might cover inappropriate use of medication, restriction of activities, use of secure accommodation or inappropriate personal care (e.g. lifting and handling or use of physical restraint inappropriately). Additionally it could include exclusion from services, deprivation of contact with families and friends, teasing or harassment or wearing of inappropriate clothes.

The right to have private and family life respected (Article 8) could be violated by the provision of personal care provided in an inappropriate way and safeguarded by the provision of appropriate family support services. This right includes the right to recognition of cultural, religious and social preferences of the individual.

The Human Rights Act strengthens the rights of children and parents to be involved in decision-making and reduces discrimination by strengthening access to existing services for people with disabilities. It covers all services and has major implications for access to health, social care, leisure, housing etc.

According to the British Institute of Learning Disabilities (BILD) those who have a concern about the violation of human rights of a person with intellectual disabilities should:

- Take the person's concerns seriously

- Seek advice from a social services care manager or a member of the local community intellectual disabilities team

- Seek advice or help from a local self-advocacy or citizen advocacy group

- Contact the Social Services Inspection Team or local service user and patient forums (see below) to find out about local complaints procedures. Contact details will be in the local phone book

A member of staff supporting somebody with intellectual disabilities can:

- Ensure they know about human rights and the Human Rights Act

- Question care practices in their organization to ensure they do not violate human rights

- Ensure that they get appropriate training and support

- Ensure that they know about the organization's 'whistle blowing' policy (in other words, what to do if they think something happening at work is wrong and they want to tell other people about it)

The NHS Plan (2000) called for the abolition of Community Health Councils. From January 2003, patient forums exist in each NHS Trust. Each forum is drawn from a mix of service users and local representatives of patient and voluntary organizations. Its function is to monitor and review the range and operation of services and how well they operate. The forums will have the freedom to report their recommendations to the trust and any other body they think is appropriate.

The Disability Discrimination Act[1] (1995)

The Disability Discrimination Act (1995) makes it unlawful for service providers or employers to discriminate against someone with a disability. The term 'disability' is defined as a physical or mental impairment that has a substantial or long-term effect on the person's ability to perform day-to-day activities. Such abilities include speech, hearing, and the ability to remember, to perceive danger or to concentrate. 'Mental impairment' covers intellectual disabilities and mental health problems, but mental health is only covered when it relates to a 'clinically recognized condition'. The disabled person must have this condition for at least 12 months or have a condition which is likely to recur to be protected under the Act. A disability that has been established as such in the past is covered even if the symptoms are not currently present.

In employment, the Act safeguards the rights of the person in terms of discrimination in recruitment and if the contract is ended. The employer is responsible for making adjustments that help the person to overcome the effects of their disability and time off should be granted to attend medical appointments. To be effective applications under the Disability Discrimination Act can be made up to three months from the alleged act of discrimination.

The Act also provides protection against disability discrimination in access to goods and services, land and property, education, and transport. These areas have an impact on service providers for people with disabilities and mental health problems.

Physical interventions: policy and ethical framework[2]

Recent research has shown that 50 per cent of people with intellectual disabilities, emotional or behavioural difficulties and challenging behaviour will have physical interventions used on them at some point in their life. Such interventions should be carried out within a legal and ethical framework that safeguards the person with intellectual disabilities and staff.

Physical interventions have been defined in the British Institute of Learning Disabilities (BILD) guidance as:

> A method of responding to the challenging behaviour of people with intellectual disabilities and/or autism which involves some degree of direct physical force which limits or restricts the movement or mobility of the person concerned.

The BILD policy framework for physical interventions has set out three categories of physical intervention:

1. Direct physical contact between staff and a service user, e.g. holding a person's arms and legs to stop them attacking someone

2. The use of barriers (e.g. locked doors) to limit freedom of movement, e.g. placing door catches or bolts beyond the reach of service users

3. Materials or equipment which restrict or prevent movement, e.g. placing splints on a person's arms to restrict movement

Physical interventions should be used in the context of other strategies for the person, after other less intrusive methods have been tried and found to be unsuccessful, and as a part of individual management plans.

Managers in services have a responsibility for the development of policies on the appropriate use of physical interventions, and for ensuring that staff are appropriately trained and work in ways that are consistent with the law. Good practice should involve the following:

- Staff should always record the use of physical interventions fully and honestly

- Emergency responses to behaviours and follow-up process required should be clearly laid out

- Service users should be involved as much as possible in developing the physical interventions policy of the organization

- Staff training and support is essential to ensure good practice in the use of physical interventions

Notes

1   For more information see the British Institute for Learning Disabilities (BILD) website.
2   For more information see the BILD website.

Resources

British Institute of Learning Disabilities (BILD)
Campion House
Green Street
Kidderminster
Worcestershire DY10 1JL
Tel: 01562 723010
Fax: 01562 723029
Website: www.bild.org.uk
Email: enquiries@bild.org.uk

(Provides information, fact sheets, publications and training and consultancy services for organizations and individuals)

BILD Easy Guide to Physical Interventions

(A summary can be obtained from the BILD website: www.bild.org.uk/factsheets/physical_interventions.htm.)

Physical Interventions – A Policy Framework. by J. Harris, D. Allen, M. Cornick, A. Jefferson and R. Mills (1996) Kidderminster: BILD.
(A summary can be obtained from the BILD website)

Citizens Advice Bureau
National Association of Citizens Advice Bureaux
Myddleton House
115-123 Pentonville Road
London N1 9LZ
Website: www.nacab.org.uk

(Provides an Advice Guide, offering up-to-dae, independent advice, at
www.adviceguide.org.uk)

The Department for Constitutional Affairs: Mental Capacity
Website: www.dca.gov.uk/incapacity/index.htm

(Simple guidance on current law, including information about mental incapacity laws)

Disability Rights Commission
Freepost MID02164
Stratford-upon-Avon CV37 9BR
Tel: 08457 622633
Website: www.drc-gb.org

(Provides an advice and information service: independent body established by an Act
of Parliament to eliminate discrimination against disabled people and to promote
equality of opportunity)

European Court of Human Rights
Website: www.echr.coe.int

(Detailing decisions of the European Court of Human Rights)

'Free thinking' *Society Guardian* article (February 2001)
Website: http://society.guardian.co.uk/humanrights/story/0,7991,434316,00.html

(Details importance of an accessible guide to human rights for people with intellectual
disabilities)

Human Rights Unit Helpdesk
Department for Constitutional Affairs
Home Office
50 Queen Anne's Gate
London SW1H 9AT
Tel: 020 7210 1437
Website: www.dca.gov.uk/hract
Email: humanrights@dca.gsi.gov.uk

HyperGuide: Mental Health Act
Website: www.hyperguide.co.uk/mha/index.htm

(A website providing a basic guide to mental health law – the Mental Health Act
1983)

Liberty
21 Tabard Street
London SE1 4LA
Tel: 020 7403 3888
Website: www.liberty-human-rights.org.uk

(Providing advice and information about human rights and civil liberties)

Mental Health Care

Website: www.mentalhealthcare.org.uk

(Information about mental illness and the latest research from the South London and Maudsley NHS Trust and the Institute of Psychiatry. The site currently deals with schizophrenia and bipolar disorder and is particularly suited to carers, friends and family of anyone with a mental illness.)

Public Guardianship Office

Archway Tower
2 Junction Road
London N19 5SZ
Tel: 020 7664 7000 or 0845 330 2900
Website: www.publictrust.gov.uk

(Offering forms and publications: provides financial protection services for clients who are not able to manage their financial affairs because of mental incapacity)

Study Guide: Human Rights Act 1998

By The General Council of The Bar (2000) Home Office Communication Directorate.

(Study Guide and Introduction free to download from www.crimereduction.gov.uk/hra.htm)

Chapter 7

Autism[1]

Mary Jane Spiller and Anastasia Gratsa

Key messages from this chapter

What is autism?

What causes autism?

Recent research

Diagnosis of autism

The process of assessment

How does autism affect people?

What may happen long term?

Additional emotional and behavioural problems

Therapeutic interventions

How can you help the person you care for?

Resources

Key messages from this chapter

- The cause of autism is unknown. It affects the person throughout life.
- Individuals with autism have difficulties in interpersonal relationships, and verbal and non-verbal communication

---

continued...

problems. Rituals and fixed behaviours, compulsive actions and rigid routines for daily activities are common.

- Many people with autism have intellectual disabilities and also additional emotional and behavioural problems (e.g. anxiety and mood disturbance, disruptive and self-absorbed behaviour).

- Autism changes over time. During adulthood the majority of people with autism and intellectual disabilities are likely to require some level of support.

- Different kinds of therapeutic interventions include psychological and social interventions and techniques that manage behaviour. These lead to a reduction in difficult behaviour and increase social and communication skills.

What is autism?

Autism is a development disability that affects someone's emotional, social and mental development. It acts as a vulnerability factor for someone developing a mental health problem. It consists of a set of features that must be present for the condition to be diagnosed. The condition varies from person to person. Some people have accompanying intellectual disabilities whereas others are of average or above average intelligence. The core features of autism include impairment in three main areas:

1. Social interaction: people with autism have difficulties in interpreting social behaviour which affects their ability to interact with others

2. Communication: people with autism are affected in their ability to use everyday non-verbal and verbal communication, some are mute, and others have complex speech

3. Thinking and behaving in a flexible way: people with autism often have restricted, repetitive and fixed (stereotyped) behaviours, interests and activities

These features may change throughout life and behaviour problems can range from severe to milder impairments. In this chapter we have tried to give an overview of all the main issues and problems that you might be faced with if you care for someone with autism. We hope it will help you to feel empowered to participate in the management plan of the person you care for.

A mother of a 37-year-old man with autism said:

> My son was always interested in carpentry since he was little. But we didn't know he was autistic. He was helping sweeping the floor or cleaning the machines in his dad's shop. He used to help at home as well. He used to love doing my bed. I wasn't allowed to do my bed; it was his job. Every day he had to do the same things, a lot of things. He used to fold the clothes and put them on the floor like little soldiers; so many things he used to do. I always told him that he was special because all people are different and praised him when he did something good. I wished I knew earlier on.
>
> Once my son went to a fast food place for something to eat and apparently he sat next to some girls. They objected and they told him to move away and he didn't because he said this was his seat, why should he move? So they pushed him and I think he pushed them back, so they phoned their boyfriends on the mobile and somebody came and chased him. Then this man started hitting my son. Since that day I noticed that his behaviour changed, he became more aggressive. He started fighting with his brothers because he wanted things. You know, he kept saying 'I want to go out', 'Why should I be different?', he kept crying and he started turning over the furniture.

What causes autism?

The cause of autism is unknown. It is probably not due to just one specific cause but a number of causes acting together. Autism in people with intellectual disabilities usually becomes obvious within the first 30 months of life and it affects the person throughout life. Sometimes, however, people are not diagnosed until they reach school, or even adulthood.

Recent research

Autism is 3 to 4 times more common in men than women. There is also an increased likelihood if there is a family history of autism, intellectual problems, speech delays, aloofness and social eccentricity, obsessional behaviours and depression.

It has been suggested that the occurrence of autism is increasing. This may be because awareness and assessment methods for autism have improved in the last few years.

Scientists are looking for links between specific environmental characteristics and information that each of us carries in our genes, which might make some individuals more susceptible to autism than others. They are also trying to understand why there is so much variation in the symptoms between individuals who suffer from autism.

Diagnosis of autism

Autism usually emerges in early infancy, but the diagnosis of autism remains especially difficult before two years of age when language skills become more obvious.

In order to diagnose autism professionals will look for delays or abnormal functioning in the following areas starting before the age of three years:

1. Social interaction

2. Language as used in social communication

3. Symbolic or imaginative play

Some people talk about **autistic spectrum disorders** to reflect the variation in severity that different people show in each of these three areas. This spectrum is seen as a continuum from a person who is aloof and has intellectual disabilities to a person who is intelligent with poor social skills, with what is called Asperger's syndrome.

The process of assessment

Over the past forty years various ways have been developed specifically to assist in the diagnosis of autism. Because the cause of autism is unknown, diagnosis relies upon observation and description of the person's behaviour and history of development. Systematic tools for this have been developed.

The diagnosis requires a comprehensive, multi-disciplinary (more than one specialist) assessment comprising of the following:

- A developmental history (e.g. was the child delayed in speaking?)

- A family history (e.g. is there another member in the family that suffers from autism?)

- Observation of the person's behaviour and interaction with others

- A medical assessment including tests for known causes of developmental delay (e.g. chromosome analysis to detect genetic problems) and tests to check the person's hearing

- A language assessment and intelligence tests

- Specialized assessment and observational checklists for diagnosing autism, completed by a clinician, and other checklists completed by a parent/carer or teacher

After completing the assessment the individual, parents and carers are given feedback about the diagnosis as the first step in developing a plan of intervention and services required (see Chapter 4 on therapeutic interventions).

How does autism affect people?

1. Difficulties in social interaction

Individuals with autism have certain difficulties in interpersonal relationships. They may not show an interest in other people, and may appear aloof or remote. Actions that we think of as simple and often take for granted can seem like complicated interactions for someone with autism.

All people with autism show difficulties in social situations; however, the nature of these may change or get better over the years. For example, there may be an increase in interest in other people. They may be able to develop some social skills often learned in a mechanical or inflexible manner.

2. Communicating with others

Both verbal and non-verbal communication problems are often the cause for parents' and carers' concern and the reason why they seek help. About a third of people with autism and intellectual disabilities are not able to use language. Not being able to communicate with other people effectively, or to understand what others are saying or what is going on around them, can cause enormous distress and anxiety. It can also cause aggressive or disruptive behaviours, or it can make someone withdraw into ritualistic or obsessional activities. When a person with autism is able to use language, the development and usage is out of the ordinary. Often the tone of speech and the voice may sound mechanical and flat. Some speak too loudly or whisper, sometimes developing an unusual accent. Some create their own unusual words or phrases and understand metaphors in a literal sense. For example, it is possible that someone with autism will look for cats and dogs every time they hear the expression 'it's raining cats and dogs'.

A person with autism might appear to have no desire to communicate with others. They might only communicate when they need to tell someone what they want. Factual comments may also be expressed a lot, and often when they seem irrelevant to the situation. Some people with autism can talk non-stop, regardless of the situation or how others respond.

Echolalia (repetition of words or phrases heard) is very common. Some people with autism repeat advertising jingles or dialogues for no apparent reason. They are more likely to talk at you rather than with you, to intrude and talk out of context and use speech as a means to an end rather than engage in a social conversation.

Often a person with autism is able to understand more than they can actually communicate. They may become distressed or frustrated by their inability to express needs by words or gestures.

3. Imagination

People with autism usually have rigid and limited interests with an obvious lack of imagination and creativity. A person with autism can have difficulty in understanding that other people can see things from a different point of view. This means that our reactions to things can seem confusing or frightening. This can also mean that people with autism seem to behave in a way that shows no thought of the wider social effects of their actions.

4. Rituals and stereotyped (fixed) interests or behaviours

Compulsive actions, rituals and rigid routines for daily activities are common. There is often a resistance to changes in routine or the environment. The person may become extremely distressed if, for example, a new route is taken to the day centre, or the furniture in the house is rearranged. Another example is that of a young woman with autism who has to buy three of the same product every time she goes shopping. People with autism can show distress if these repetitive patterns are disrupted or interrupted. People with autism rarely involve others in their activities unless they are given a particular role in a controlled situation.

Individuals with autism are often preoccupied with fine detail of an object; a fascination with certain aspects of routines such as bus routes or train timetables is also common. They might repeatedly ask questions to which they expect only specific answers.

5. Other common linked characteristics

The following features are not specific to individuals with autism and may occur in others with intellectual disabilities. These are:

- Unusual dietary habits
- Sleep disturbance
- Abnormalities of mood
- Self-injurious behaviour
- Lack of response to pain

- Heightened sensitivity to sound
- Preoccupation with tactile stimulation

One in three children with autism and intellectual disabilities develop **epilepsy** (see Chapter 8).

What may happen long term?

Autism changes over time. Unfortunately in the young child with autism there is no way of knowing with confidence what the long-term outcome will be. Some characteristics of autism may change as the person grows older but the main social, communication and behavioural difficulties persist. Adolescence can bring the development of symptoms such as aggressive or obsessive compulsive behaviour, and an increase in anxiety, tension and mood disturbance.

During adulthood the majority of people with autism and intellectual disabilities are likely to require some level of support. It is usually those adults who can communicate that are able to live independently and remain in employment; however, some difficulties with social interaction remain. The majority of people with autism will experience behavioural, emotional and social problems throughout life, but nevertheless will improve and gradually become more independent.

Additional emotional and behavioural problems

People with autism have high levels of anxiety and mood disturbance, disruptive and self-absorbed behaviour as well as communication disturbance and social relating problems.

Anti-social behaviour

Deliberate anti-social behaviours (e.g. lying, stealing, and lighting fires) are unlikely to occur because they require social knowledge and skills that are beyond most individuals with autism. However, behaviour seen by others as anti-social may occur. For example, one young man regularly set fire to the hay shed on the family farm because he enjoyed the sight, sound and smell of the flames, not because he wanted to cause harm or distress.

Disruptive behaviour

Disruptive behaviours can lead to problems where the person lives, or if they go to a day centre. Tantrums, noisiness, impatience, aggression, self-injury and stubbornness can all be problematic.

Anxiety

People with autism often have high levels of anxiety. The symptoms of anxious behaviour include:

- Fear of separation from familiar people
- Specific fears or phobias (e.g. certain sounds, smells, objects, animals)
- Resistance to change (e.g. new clothes, food, routines)
- Panic and emotional distress for little or no apparent reason
- Tension
- Shyness
- Irritability

These symptoms of anxiety, apart from the distress they cause the individual, have the potential to disrupt education, and create management problems and stress for the parents and carers.

If the anxiety can be clearly identified then there is an opportunity for an intervention to be used to help manage it. Attention must be paid to organizing a predictable environment for the person, which can help to reduce anxiety and stress. Psychological treatments, particularly cognitive and behavioural approaches, are effective treatments. These might need to be modified if the individual cannot communicate with language. Antidepressants may also reduce anxiety.

Depression

Those with autism are at increased risk of suffering from depression. They can be irritable, have sleep and appetite problems (inducing weight loss), obsessional thoughts and preoccupations, compulsive behaviours, and thoughts of suicide. These problems can hinder education and adjustment, and interfere with the quality of life.

Depression can be treated with cognitive therapy, relaxation training and rewarding experiences. These are described in Chapter 4 on therapeutic interventions, and are usually modified according to the ability of the individual.

Antidepressant medication may be necessary if the depression is severe or persistent.

Attention deficit hyperactivity disorder

Being easily distracted, lack of concentration, impulsiveness, poor planning ability, disorganized behaviour, fidgetiness and motor overactivity are common symptoms in young people with autism but may decrease with maturity. Management requires a broad approach including planned, structured, time-limited activities in simple steps, limitation of the amount of environmental stimulation, planning for change, communication programmes (e.g. visual systems), behaviour modification, relaxation and perhaps medication.

Therapeutic interventions

There is no cure for autism. Many treatment approaches and therapies have been reported in the past often without strong evidence of benefit.

Current treatment usually consists of multi-disciplinary structured treatment programmes that incorporate special education, behavioural management, social and communication skills training and medication when indicated. Intervention must involve collaboration between the individual, family/carers and the professionals involved.

Psychosocial interventions

As with other conditions, the challenging behaviours in autism can be maintained or increased by the amount of attention or reinforcement they receive. It is important to understand that challenging behaviours that seem very similar from person to person, or even with the same person at different times, can actually have very different causes. For example, destructive and aggressive behaviours can happen for a variety of reasons such as:

- The person's frustration at not being able to communicate
- Anxiety or fear
- It being the only way they can control others around them or their environment
- A disruption in their rituals and routines

For an intervention to be successful it is therefore very important to try to work out:

- Why the behaviour occurs
- What the behaviour achieves for all people concerned
- What could be done to replace it

Many behaviour management techniques have been developed to reduce these difficult behaviours, and to help increase a person's social and communication skills.

Visual props using simple pictures and line drawings, signing systems and also photographs are often used to help people with autism communicate. Each person must be carefully assessed to determine which system will suit him or her best.

The approaches used to treat social difficulties vary according to the needs of each person with autism, in particular their level of intellectual disabilities, age and the nature of their social difficulty. Areas covered may include understanding about friends and strangers, interacting with peers, understanding rules and when they may be broken, and understanding emotions.

Detailed information about these general approaches is given in Chapter 4 on therapeutic interventions and Chapter 5 on challenging behaviour.

Biological interventions

There is no medication for autism itself. Different medicines act on the symptoms of autism (e.g. anxiety) and not on the main difficulties of social, communication and imagination functions. The use of medication should only occur as part of a comprehensive management plan that includes approaches to improving specific needs such as communication, behaviour management, education, social skills training, structuring of daily routine, and carer support.

How can you help the person you care for?

Depending on the type of autism the person has there are many things that you can do to help the person you are caring for. These can include the following:

- Try to understand that people with autism have a different way of viewing the world. Try to see situations from their point of view

- Try to value and develop the person's own interests and activities. Don't just try to change them to become more like us, as they will find this difficult and won't necessarily want to do it

- Try to create a secure, predictable and structured environment for the person to live in

- Always let the person have a clear idea of what is going to happen during the day, and use picture charts or lists as reminders

- When something is going to change or stop always give them a warning before (for example, 'When this television programme is over your friend John is coming to visit you')

- Always try to support the person when they face a change in a known routine

- Don't assume the person knows what you're going to do next and never take it for granted that they know the next step in a sequence of events

- Always say their name first before you speak to them

- Speak in short phrases and use pictures, photos or gestures to provide more information about what you want them to do

- Try to use language that is easy to understand, specific and honest. Don't use abstract language, and try to use objects to aid understanding

- Avoid sarcasm or irony as these are confusing and can be disrespectful

- Allow the person enough time to respond – giving time for the words to be recognized and considered

- Try to reduce any anxiety they might have by using a quiet and calm voice and manner

- Give the person simple choices, such as the apple or the banana, and make it clear to avoid confusion

- Always be consistent and try to be positive

Looking after an individual with autism can be very rewarding but also draining, particularly if the right support is not available. Therefore it is important that you look after your own mental health as well. (See also Chapter 9 on carers' needs and support.)

It has been shown that compliance with treatment is improved when family or carers and the person with autism are involved in regular reviews of management. It is therefore important to ensure that both you and the person you care for are involved in any reviews of management.

Notes

1   This chapter has been adapted with permission from A.V. Brereton and B.J. Tong.

2   For more information please refer to Jones, G., Jordan, R. and Morgan, H. (2001) *All About Autistic Spectrum Disorders*. London: Foundation for People with Learning Disabilities

Resources
Autism Networks
Imperial Chambers
Prince Albert Street
Crewe
Cheshire CW1 2DX
Tel: 01270 580444
Website: www.autismnetworks.org.uk

(A group of parents, carers and professionals offering support, advice and encouragement)

Centre for the Study of Autism
PO Box 4538
Salem
Oregon 97302
USA
Website: www.autism.org

(Information on autism, associated syndromes and research)

The National Autistic Society (NAS)
33 City Road
London ECIV 1NG
Tel: 0870 600 8585 or 020 7833 2299
Website: www.nas.org.uk
Email: autismhelpline@nas.org.uk

(Helpline and services for adults and children. Also provides training courses)

Tony Attwood
Website: www.tonyattwood.com.au

(A guide for professionals, families and friends of people with Asperger's syndrome and their partners with resources, messages and issues related to Asberger's syndrome)

The **Foundation for People with Learning Disabilities** has published a booklet on autism called *All About Autistic Spectrum Disorders* (see Resources section in Chapter 3 for contact details).

Chapter 8

Epilepsy

Mary Jane Spiller, Anastasia Gratsa and Geraldine Holt

Key messages from this chapter

What is epilepsy?

What is the link between epilepsy and mental health problems?

How common is epilepsy?

What are seizures?

Can epilepsy impair cognitive functioning?

Assessment and diagnosis

Therapeutic interventions

How can you help the person you care for?

Resources

Key messages from this chapter

- When someone has epilepsy they have repeated seizures, which originate in the brain. There are many types of epilepsy and over 40 types of seizure, which will affect different people in different ways.

- People with epilepsy whether they have intellectual disabilities or not are more likely to have mental health problems. Epilepsy itself is not a mental health problem. The abnormal brain

---

continued...

activity, the change in intellectual processes (knowing, thinking, learning), the emotions experienced as a result, and the possible social stigma can make someone more vulnerable to develop mental health problems.

- People with intellectual disabilities and epilepsy can have a high standard of support in the community, based on a multi-disciplinary approach. Good co-ordination between the family/carers, GPs, hospital and local authority services is essential.

- The prevention, early diagnosis and treatment of epilepsy, together with the prevention of seizures, is essential to avoid additional problems for people with intellectual disabilities. The seizures and their treatment may affect behaviour and the person's quality of life. Any intervention should aim to protect and promote the health of the person you care for as well as allowing them to be as independent as possible.

- You need to be aware of the medical issues of epilepsy. Supporting the person to accept their illness and have a fulfilling life is important in creating a more effective working relationship between you and the doctors and other professionals.

What is epilepsy?

If someone has **epilepsy** this means that they have repeated seizures. Seizures are caused by a temporary change in the way someone's brain cells work. During a seizure someone might 'black out' or have unusual feelings, thoughts or movements. It usually only lasts for a matter of seconds or minutes, but in extreme cases it can last longer. After a seizure the brain cells are able to work as normal. The old name for a seizure was 'a fit'.

Lots of people may have a single seizure during their life, but this does not mean that they have epilepsy. If someone experiences repeated seizures, then they may be diagnosed as having epilepsy.

There are many different types of epilepsy. When someone with epilepsy has a seizure it can be a 'non-convulsive seizure'. In other words, a seizure does not always involve involuntary body movements and what we might typically think of as 'fitting'.

A carer of someone with intellectual disabilities and epilepsy who has epilepsy himself talks about his experience:

> I have found post seizure time much worse than seizures. For example a grand mal attack would be followed by severe headache, painful mouth (bitten) and confusion for some hours. Auras and feelings after partial seizures might sound easy to deal with but at a young age I was very confused by this sort of déjà vu experience, which caused me a lot of stress and anxiety. I feel that carers need to know more detail about epilepsy and possibly First Aid if the cared-for person is not able to explain him or herself. Sometimes there are no known triggers found. Carers should be encouraged to find out more details about pre, during and post seizure action that they may need to be aware of.

What is the link between epilepsy and mental health problems?

People with epilepsy whether they have intellectual disabilities or not are more likely to have mental health problems than those who do not have epilepsy. Epilepsy itself is not a mental health problem. The association between the two can be thought of in a combination of biological, psychological and social terms (see also Chapter 1). The abnormal brain activity and the medications used to control it (biological component) may predispose to mental health problems. The change in intellectual processes and the emotional response to them (psychological component) may act as vulnerability factors as may stigmatization and exclusion from society (social component).

How common is epilepsy?

The frequency of epilepsy occurring in people with intellectual disabilities is higher than in the rest of the population. About 30 per cent of people with intellectual disabilities also have epilepsy. The more severe the intellectual disability the more likely it is that the person will also have epilepsy.

At least 50 per cent of people with severe intellectual disabilities also have epilepsy.

Epilepsy starting later in life in people with Down syndrome may be linked to dementia.

What are seizures?

There are many different types of epilepsy and about 40 different types of seizures. Seizures affect people in different ways. The symptoms of a seizure (what people experience) depend on where the change in brain activity takes place, and how widely and quickly it spreads.

The medical names given to different types of seizures have changed over recent years so you might hear different names. There are two main types of seizures: **generalized seizures** and **partial seizures**.

Generalized seizures involve the whole brain and affect both sides of the body at the same time. Consciousness is impaired so the person will have no memory of the seizure. They often occur with no warning. There are several types of generalized seizures such as tonic-clonic (old term: grand mal), myoclonic, atonic, and absence (old term: petit mal).

There are many possible causes or **triggers** of a seizure, and they vary from person to person. Seizures can often come without warning but some general factors that can make them more likely include:

- Drinking too much alcohol
- Stressful events
- Flickering lights
- Not having enough sleep
- Skipping meals and eating an unbalanced diet
- Illness

Identifying any factors that trigger a seizure can be very useful, as then situations where seizures might occur can be avoided.

In a **partial seizure** the change in brain activity starts in just one part of the brain. It can stay in the same place or spread to the rest of the brain. Partial brain seizures can be **simple** or **complex**.

When someone has a **simple partial seizure** they may complain of butterflies in their stomach, tingling or other feelings and emotions. These are called auras. There is no loss of consciousness and the person is able to answer questions.

In **complex partial seizures**, there is some impairment of consciousness. There may be strange behaviours, such as lip smacking, chewing, fiddling with clothes and the person may seem to be in a trance. This abnormal brain activity may spread to other areas of the brain, resulting in a secondary generalized seizure.

Can epilepsy impair cognitive functioning?

Cognitive functioning is the mental processes of knowing, thinking and learning. People who have intellectual disabilities have problems in these three areas usually due to the underlying brain damage rather than the epilepsy itself. If the seizures are well controlled and the medication regime is kept simple further difficulties with cognitive functioning are less likely to occur. If seizures are poorly controlled or very frequent they may affect the person's overall quality of life. If seizures are controlled better these difficulties may also improve.

Assessment and diagnosis[1]

Doctors can find it difficult to diagnose epilepsy as there is not one particular test to use and many other things could be the cause of the symptoms. Also, when someone is not having a seizure his or her brain cells may behave as normal. The person might not be conscious during the seizure so they might not have any memory of it.

The diagnosis of epilepsy in people with intellectual disabilities can be especially difficult. The person may be unable to give a clear account of their symptoms because they have no memory of the seizure, or because they find them difficult to explain. In such cases, the doctor may rely on descriptions you give and gather information by getting to know the person, and speaking to other informants/carers.

During the assessment the doctor will ask you and the person you care for many questions. He or she will need to know how many seizures the person has had and whether there is any history of epilepsy in the family. The doctor must be told about any medication the person is taking.

The doctor may ask how the person felt before the seizure, such as whether they were hungry, thirsty, tired, cold, dizzy or felt sick, or whether they had unusual chest pains. The doctor will need to know if the person had drunk any alcoholic drinks before the seizure, and whether there were any warning signs. The doctor will also ask about how the person felt after the seizure, and whether they had hurt themselves at all.

The doctor will ask you questions that the person who had the seizure might not be able to answer. For example, what the person was doing before the seizure, and what exactly happened during the seizure. The doctor will want to know how long the seizure lasted, and whether the person seemed confused.

Information about the person's past medical history and behaviour can help. Aggression, bizarre behaviour, abnormal movements, the side effects of medication and self-injurious behaviour may all be part of the person's everyday behaviour without the presence of epilepsy. However, such features may also be present in epilepsy.

You and the person you care for might have many questions that you want the doctor to answer. For example:

- 'What sort of epilepsy does the person have?'
- 'Why do you think it has developed now?'
- 'Will they always have it?'
- 'What tests are you recommending and what are you looking for?'
- 'How will you treat the epilepsy?'
- 'Is there anything we can do to reduce the side effects of any treatment?'
- 'What will happen if the treatment doesn't work?'
- 'Is there anything that they can't/shouldn't do?'

- 'What can we do to prevent the seizures?'
- 'Where can we get more information about epilepsy?'

Therapeutic interventions

Medical treatment of seizures in people with intellectual disabilities is the same as for people without intellectual disabilities. However, it might be more difficult to achieve control over the seizures. The seizures may also be more severe and more frequent.

Often a person with intellectual disabilities and epilepsy has physical disabilities and mental health problems. The stigma associated with disability can cause the person to have low self-esteem and bring about psychological problems.

A comprehensive assessment of social (e.g. culture, interests and lifestyle), environmental (e.g. stress) and medical aspects of the person's life (e.g. past and present medical history, sensory problems, special medical conditions) is necessary to determine an appropriate intervention plan.

Recording of seizures and ongoing events is also very important in order to determine the nature of the epilepsy and its causes (e.g. when the seizures started, how long they lasted for, how frequent they were etc.) and to monitor the effectiveness of any interventions made.

Biological interventions

There are many different types of medication available now to help manage epilepsy, and the carefully planned use of these is very important for controlling the seizures. The doctor will try to find the most suitable medication and dose to prescribe.

Different types of anti-epileptic medication (also known as anticonvulsants) treat different types of epilepsy. The basic principles of treatment are the same as for people without intellectual disabilities.

Medication is started at a low dose and slowly increased to a dose which controls the epilepsy. However, if it is severe epilepsy then more than one type of medication might be needed. Withdrawal of medication should be done gradually, as stopping the medication suddenly can cause uncontrolled seizures.

It is important that you keep a record of seizures and that you bring this to the clinic. It may be that seizures tend to occur at a particular time. Medication can be altered to overcome this. Some women experience increased seizures around periods and may need extra medication at this time.

The combination of anti-epileptic medication with antipsychotics or antidepressants (see Chapter 4 on therapeutic interventions) can increase seizures. However, it may be necessary in order to treat a mental health problem or help control behaviour. In such cases the doctor will consider prescribing a higher dose of anticonvulsants.

Some medicines that you can buy over the counter such as cold cures, and medicines to treat hay fever, interact with anti-epileptic drugs. You should therefore always check with the chemist or the doctor before buying non-prescription medicines.

BLOOD TESTS

Monitoring with blood tests (to check the level of medication in the blood) may be useful in controlling seizures and controlling side effects. Some types of medication can only work if they are at certain concentration levels in the blood stream (e.g. phenytoin) and blood tests can help to decide the dose of medication to be taken. Some types of medication have side effects when the level of medication in the blood is too high (e.g. carbamazepine). With stable epilepsy, some doctors advise an annual check of blood levels but this is not necessary with all types of anti-epileptic medication.

Saliva testing may be possible as an alternative to blood testing for some people.

It is essential that the medication is taken correctly as prescribed by the doctor. Seek advice from the doctor immediately if the person you care for starts to have more seizures than usual. You should also get advice if the person is unable to take their medication for some reason, for example if they have a stomach upset, or if any other aspect of their health changes.

Anti-epileptic medication can lead to drowsiness and poor concentration. Newer types of medication are less likely to do this.

TYPES OF MEDICATION

Below are the more commonly used types of anti-epileptic medication and their more common side effects described in alphabetical order. This is not an exhaustive list but should help you gain some understanding of the main issues.

Carbamazepine (brand name: Tegretol)

Carbamazepine is used to treat many forms of epilepsy. It is also used in manic depression, challenging behaviour and facial pain. Side effects include generalized rash, which goes away when the medicine is stopped. Some people suffer from nausea and vomiting. If dizziness, drowsiness, double vision, fever, sore throat, bruising or bleeding occurs the doctor needs to be consulted immediately. However, this medicine is usually without any serious side effects. Blood tests are not necessary.

Diazepam (brand name: Stesolid)

Diazepam is used rectally and sometimes intravenously to control status epilepticus, which is the term used when seizures are prolonged and multiple. This is a medical emergency. For side effects see Chapter 'Benzodiazepines' section.

Ethosuximide (brand name: Zarontin)

Ethosuximide is the drug of choice in absence seizures. It may cause nausea, vomiting and drowsiness, which can be reduced by slowly introducing the drug. It can also cause behavioural disturbances. If persistent fever, sore throat, mouth ulcers, bruising or bleeding develops, contact the doctor immediately. Drug levels should be checked by blood tests.

Gabapentin (brand name: Neurontin)

Gabapentin is added to other anti-epileptic drugs to treat partial seizures. Common side effects include drowsiness, dizziness and unsteadiness. Headache, double vision, tremor, nausea and vomiting can also occur. Checking of drug levels by blood tests is not necessary.

Lamotrogine (brand name: Lamictal)

Lamotrogine is used to control partial seizures and some sorts of generalized seizures. Rash is a common side effect; the likelihood of occurrence can be reduced with slow introduction of the drug. Headache, nausea and vomiting, double vision and unsteadiness can also occur. Although rare, if there is a rash, fever, flu-like symptoms and a worsening of epilepsy, contact the doctor immediately. Checking of drug levels by blood tests is unnecessary.

Phenytoin (brand name: Epanutin)

Phenytoin is a very effective drug used to control tonic-clonic, simple and partial seizures. It is being replaced by newer medicines with fewer unwanted effects. As with most anti-epileptic drugs, clients may feel sleepy. It is important to watch out for signs that the concentration of the drug in the blood stream is too high. The person may feel dizzy, have double vision, have a headache or be off-balance when he or she tries to walk. Frequency of seizures may increase dramatically. People who have been on phenytoin for many years may develop some unattractive side effects, namely coarsening of facial features, acne-like rash and growth of gums. The level of the drug in the blood must be maintained at a certain level; therefore drug levels should be checked by blood tests.

Sodium valproate (brand name: Epilim)

Sodium valproate is effective against all forms of epilepsy. It is generally well tolerated, although sedation can occur. Some people suffer with nausea, vomiting or heartburn. Increased appetite and weight gain is a common problem. Rarely, hair loss occurs but this recovers when the drug is stopped. At high doses, tremor may occur. Very rarely, sodium valproate damages the liver. The client may feel unwell and be jaundiced (skin acquires a yellow tinge); seizure control may be lost. It is advisable to contact a doctor immediately. Blood level monitoring is not necessary.

Topiramate (brand name: Topamax)

This is used as add-on therapy for partial seizures. Sedation and nausea are common side effects. Blood level monitoring is not necessary.

Vigabatrin (brand name: Sabril)

Vigabatrin is used in chronic epilepsy not satisfactorily controlled by other anti-epileptics. It is used to treat complex partial seizures and tonic-clonic seizures. Sleepiness is a common side effect. Some people develop behavioural disturbances including irritability, nervousness, depression and aggression. Rarely, they may become psychotic.

Having intellectual disabilities does not exclude a person from brain surgery to improve their seizure control. Surgery is not suitable for everyone who has epilepsy. It may be a possibility for some of those people whose seizures are not controlled with drugs. The benefits and the possible adverse effects of surgery upon each individual are considered carefully before a decision is taken.

Psychosocial interventions

People with intellectual disabilities and epilepsy may experience difficulties in psychosocial functioning, particularly in interpersonal relationships.

The impact of epilepsy, as well as intellectual disabilities and mental health difficulties, can produce problems. These may present in the form of poorly controlled seizures, the person not wanting to take medication, or changes in behaviour. Support and counselling can help the individual to accept the illness. Mental health professionals will work in the context of consent, health education, and an understanding of the person's values, concepts of illness, abilities and developmental level.

It is very important for the person to understand and learn to cope with any limitations caused by epilepsy. The person may resist this by denying that they even have epilepsy, or may put all the responsibility on family and carers. An overprotective environment may strengthen this. It is important to provide a caring environment that is safe but helpful to self-development and independence. This will include assessment of possible risk in areas such as activities and self-administration of medication etc.

Psychological treatment can help to improve seizure control and possibly the reduction of medication. In addition, behavioural techniques, including relaxation, have been shown to be of value (see Chapter 4 on therapeutic interventions).

Psychological interventions are not intended to replace medication. They should be used in addition to the biological intervention. Prescribed medicines should not be stopped without proper consultation with the doctor.

How can you help the person you care for?[2]

For the assessment

The doctor will need information about the person's medical history. Also, try to collect as much information as possible regarding the seizures (before, during and after), especially if the person cannot remember or if he or she is unable to explain. You might be asked to provide similar information (e.g. ongoing events) to other mental health professionals in order to determine the nature of seizures and if possible the triggers.

Write down what questions you might want the doctor to answer and arrange for a longer appointment if you feel you need more time to go through your questions (see also section on assessment and diagnosis earlier in this chapter).

After the assessment

Support the person you care for to accept the limitations posed by epilepsy. This can be achieved by encouraging him or her to have a full programme of activities that he or she enjoys. This will help the person to develop life skills and promote self-esteem. A well-balanced caring environment that allows and encourages self-development and independence can help to promote good mental health and possibly better control over seizures. Therefore try and support the person to make their own informed choices about things that are important to them.

Note

1   More information is available from the Epilepsy Action website: www.epilepsy.org.uk/intro/diagnosis/html

Resources

About Epilepsy is a pack designed with and for people with mild to moderate intellectual disabilities. It contains eight leaflets about different aspects of living with epilepsy, including safety, medication, EEG and MRI. The pack uses words, symbols and photos and is available from the National Society for Epilepsy (NSE) online shop (see website address below).

Epilepsy Action (also known as the British Epilepsy Association)
New Anstey House
Gate Way Drive
Yeadon
Leeds LS19 7NW
Freephone helpline: 0800 800 5050 (9am–4.30pm Mon to Thurs, 9am–4pm Fri)
Website: www.epilepsy.org.uk
Email helpline: helpline@epilepsy.org.uk
Email: epilepsy@epilepsy.org.uk

The National Society for Epilepsy (NSE)
Chesham Lane
Chalfont St Peter
Bucks SL9 0RJ
Tel: 01494 601300
Fax: 01494 871927
Website: www.epilepsynse.org.uk

UK Epilepsy Helpline
Tel: 01494 601400 (10am–4pm, Monday to Friday)

The helpline is available to anyone who wants to use it – people with epilepsy, their families, friends, carers, employers, GPs, nurses, healthcare professionals, schools and students.

Chapter 9

Carers' Needs and Support

Anastasia Gratsa

Key messages from this chapter

- Carers need practical and emotional support. Carers may need help to maintain their own physical and emotional health.
- If you care for someone with intellectual disabilities and mental health problems you are entitled to an assessment of your caring, emotional, mental health and physical needs.

---

continued...

- You can contact social services to ask for such an assessment. They will provide information about other local organizations that offer help and support to you and the person you care for.

- Care giving can be difficult at times depending on the nature and extent of the needs of the person you care for. Carers are often faced with stress, anxiety and tiredness due to sleeplessness and isolation, alongside financial and practical difficulties.

- Self-help groups through local caring organizations are available to promote the well-being of carers.

Introduction

Caring for someone with intellectual disabilities and mental health can be a complex role. Sometimes carers of people with intellectual disabilities and mental health problems carry out practical tasks such as shopping and cooking alongside supporting and encouraging the person they care for.

Carers need practical and emotional support. Some of the information included in this chapter is relevant to carers in general be they parents, family members, partners, relatives or friends. It is not necessarily specific to carers of those with intellectual disabilities.

A mother of a young man with autism explains the way she has coped over the years:

> To be a good mother is hard work. It involves sleepless nights, aches and pains and friction at times with your partner and friction with the other children. You sometimes find the other children miss out on things because this child is unfortunate and you have to spend extra time, which is natural, caring for that child. The family unit is very valuable but in order to maintain it the mother and even the father must have an outlet. You cannot just take on this child and keep this problem to yourself because it stresses you when you don't have the answers to problems; when the doctors don't have the answers; as much as they are trying. Try and find yourself someone preferably who has a child with the same problem, a friend even, someone you can relate to. Even if you feel like crying you can go to that person's house, and this is very, very important; even once a week that you can go and have tea or coffee and just pour out. It is even better than medication because you see what this actually does

to you; you unwind your hurt, because as a mother you are confessing to another mother. You let out your distress, your grief and your anxieties. You don't know where the added strength came from but nature just takes over, so one must have an outlet to talk. That is very valuable in order to continue to care for your child. Some people don't have that outlet and this might cause the parent to have a nervous breakdown because it's such hard work. It is nice to have someone where you don't feel embarrassed about telling. Sometimes people are embarrassed to cry, but it doesn't hurt to get it out of your system even though at the same time having this child has made me a better person. I have become a caring person. He has carved my life and made me more aware of people hurting.

It is important for you to know what help is available. People might not be aware of what is on offer or their statutory rights. There is a great amount of information, but sometimes it can be confusing even for professionals in this field.

Who is a carer?

There are certain definitions of carers according to the Department of Health, UK Government legislation and local authority or social services policy. The definitions below provide a general guide to the different terms.

Carer

A carer is someone who cares for a relative or friend, who has a disability, an illness or a mental health problem, and provides substantial care on a regular basis. The word 'carer' does not mean care worker or care staff of any kind who are paid to provide care as part of a contract of employment.

Parents and family carers

Parents will often see themselves as parents rather than carers. If their child has additional care needs they may be entitled to additional services. Equally there are family carers (foster parents, siblings or relatives) who have important roles.

Care worker, care staff, professional carer, paid carer
These terms refer to carers who are paid to provide care as part of employment.

Service user, user
A general term that is used nowadays to refer to patients, clients or consumers of specialist services.

In this publication we are concentrating on **parents**, **family carers** and **carers**.

Assessment of the carer's ability[1]
Under the Carers (Recognition and Services) Act (1995) the social services must assess the ability of any person caring for a client. Despite the word 'services' in the title of this Act, the authority is not required to provide any services to the carer. The intention of the Act is to ensure that voluntary carers (including young children looking after sick parents) are monitored by, and their efforts supplemented by, social services provisions.

When making an assessment of a client's needs social workers/care managers must listen to the carer's view and consider the role that he or she can play. These are also called Joint Assessments.

What services should carers expect?

Carers often need help to maintain their own physical and emotional health. There are nearly *5.7 million* carers in the UK.

If you look after a relative or friend who needs support because of age, physical or intellectual disabilities or illness, including mental illness, you have a right to have your own health needs met. This chapter outlines some of the key policies and organizations that will help you in doing this. When you contact national organizations like the ones listed at the end of this chapter they should be able to provide details of the local support groups within the area where you live. You can also gain access to the organizations and use the internet by visiting your local library. Most libraries provide support for using the internet and it is free of charge but you may have to book in advance.

National Service Framework for Mental Health

If you care for someone with intellectual disabilities and mental health problems you are entitled to an assessment of your needs.

In 1999 the UK Government published the National Service Framework for Mental Health, which also applies to those who have intellectual disabilities and mental health needs. This sets out national standards and service models for treatment and care in mental health.

It says that if you regularly care for someone who has a mental health problem then every year local services should find out whether or not you have any special requirements due to your role as a carer.

The Carer's Act

In 1996 a new Carer's Act came into force. The Act emphasizes the importance of carers, and recognizes that carers have needs in addition to those of the people they look after.

If you help someone with bathing, toileting, dressing, cooking or cleaning, shopping, doing their paperwork, paying bills or just keeping someone company and taking them out then you are a carer. The Act says that you are entitled to a **Carer Assessment** if you provide regular and substantial care. To be a carer you do not have to live in the same household as the person you care for.

What is a Carer Assessment?

During a Carer Assessment you will be asked about what you do for the person you care for and about personal or health issues you might have. An assessment aims to find out if there are any services that could help you, and different options will be discussed with you and with the person you care for.

As a carer you can request an assessment of your needs at the same time as the assessment of the person you care for, or at a later time when their needs change or are reviewed. Confidential assessments are offered on request if there are difficulties or conflicts with the person you care for. Everything will be written down and it should be available for you to read and check. It will tell you if any services have been offered, and any other help you may need. It will list all the tasks you do for the person you care for and other details discussed during the assessment.

For people who cannot understand the language, interpreters are usually provided and similarly support is available for people who have a visual or hearing impairment.

You can contact social services to ask for such an assessment. The telephone number of your local council social services department will be found in your telephone directory under local authority and community information, or you can speak to your GP.

All carers are individuals and your local council may provide any service to you that will help you care or help you maintain your well-being. You may have some ideas of your own about services that would help you that you want to talk through with social services. Other services that you might want to discuss with them are those that may help the person you look after. Also, your local social services department will tell you about other organizations that offer help and support to carers and users.

Some issues you may want to think about before you undergo a Carer Assessment:[2]

- Do you get enough sleep?
- Is your health affected in other ways?
- Are you able to get out and about?
- Do you get any time for yourself?
- Are your other relationships affected?
- Do you want information about benefits?
- Are you worried you may have to give up work?
- Is the person you care for getting enough help?
- What sort of services might help you?
    - Services that give you a break

- ○ Emotional support from other carers or people who understand
- ○ Help with household tasks
- ○ Help with caring tasks during the day/night
- ○ Benefits advice
- ○ Activities for the person you care for
- Local or national support organizations you could contact
- Other help you could get
- Any charges for services
- What to do if you wish to complain

National Carers Strategy: Caring for Carers

Caring for Carers is a new strategy for carers launched by the Government at the beginning of 1999 and it is also known as the **National Carers Strategy**. Supporting carers in the valued work they do is one way of helping those that carers are caring for. All organizations involved with caring must now concentrate on the user and in doing so also include the carer.

This new Government approach to carers has three focus areas, although of course there are other areas of caring that are also important:

- **Information:** good health information on long-term care services should be available for you through the internet and NHS Direct.

- **Support:** you should be advised and actively involved in planning and providing services. Therefore, services should consult with local caring organizations

- **Care:** local authorities will be required to provide services for you and special grants will be available to help you take a break. Types of breaks for carers are identified and they include holidays, evening, day-time, night-time and Sunday sitting, as well as respite short breaks that give the opportunity for carers to pursue religious activities, hobbies, leisure etc.

Issues such as housing conditions, employment and social and emotional support can affect your health. Emotional support and assistance from family members and support groups can help you to manage stress levels, increase your sense of being in control and have a positive impact on your mental well-being.

Also, training in areas such as manual handling and lifting can reduce the risk of physical injuries. Social workers, primary care teams and GPs are responsible for identifying carers in their catchment area in order to be able to offer them appropriate help. Other areas of training give the opportunity for you to enrich your life and can increase your confidence and develop your skills, so that you can return to work if you wish, once your caring responsibilities end.

Most departments in social services are under a lot of pressure, due to a number of reasons, e.g. lack of time, heavy case loads, lack of resources and funding, and crises coming up every day and other things which have to take priority. It cannot be ignored that carers do have rights and care managers have a statutory duty to offer a Carer Assessment if the carer agrees.

Care managers/social workers have a duty to support carers as it helps to support the client; supporting the carer is good practice. An example of this is:

> Nadia has moderate intellectual disabilities. She lives at home with her father who has been providing care for Nadia for over ten years. He needs a hip replacement and his health is getting worse. He cannot do much around the house any more. Nadia has basic living skills. Nadia's care manager assessed Nadia's needs as well as her father's. Support has been put in for six weeks only to help around the house, to support Nadia's father. This was paid out of the carer's grant. It was the only thing Nadia's care manager could do. The next plan was to put in support for Nadia, by an outside carer coming in during the week to help enable and support Nadia to learn skills around the house, such as cooking and cleaning. This in fact helped Nadia's father but also enabled Nadia to enhance her day-to-day living skills.

Carers and employment

The Government has also introduced a strategy for carers in employment. This involves:

- New legislation to allow authorities to address carers' needs
- Time spent caring entitling carers to a second pension
- The Government is consulting on proposals, but by 2005 carers could receive an extra £50 a week in today's terms
- Reducing council tax for more disabled people being cared for
- Support for neighbourhood services, including carers' centres
- Considering scope for extending help to carers to return to work
- A new census confronting incomplete information about carers
- Special funding for breaks for carers

The strategy proposes that a Carers Grant will be made available to local authorities to help give support to carers. Part of the conditions of the Carers Grant is a formal requirement to produce a plan, which should describe how and what improved outcomes for users and carers will be delivered through the introduction of additional services to give carers a break from caring. Also, these plans should set out some indicators to evaluate progress.

What can carers do to help themselves?

Care giving can be difficult at times depending on the nature and extent of the needs of the person you care for. Carers are often faced with stress, anxiety, tiredness due to sleeplessness, and isolation, alongside financial and practical difficulties.

Carers need to speak out and make care managers/social workers aware of their own needs. They need to be persistent in order to make sure that they get the right kind of support that they need.

Sharing the task of caring with another person (family, relatives and friends) can often be of a great help. It is important for you to seek help when and if you need to in order to continue caring.

There are different ways that can help you to develop effective coping strategies should you need to. Self-help groups and support groups through local caring organizations are available to promote your well-being.

Notes

1   For more information see Brayne, H. and Martin, G. (1999) *Law for Social Workers*. Sixth edition. London: Stanley Thornes Publishers.

2   The Department of Health (1999), 'Caring About Carers', www.careers.gov.uk

Resources

Carers Online (Part of Carers UK)
20/25 Glasshouse Yard
London EC1A 4JT
Tel: 020 7490 8818
Fax: 020 7490 8824
Email: info@ukcarers.org
Website: www.carersonline.org.uk

Contact a Family
209–211 City Road
London EC1V 1JN
Tel: 020 7608 8700
Fax: 020 7608 8701
Minicom: 020 7608 8702
Helpline: 0808 808 3555
Website: www.cafamily.org.uk

(Contact a Family is a UK charity, which helps families who care for children with any disability or special need. Information about rare disorders and assistance to affected adults and children is offered.)

Crossroads – Caring for Carers
Crossroads Association
10 Regent Place
Rugby
Warwickshire CV21 2PN
Tel: 01788 573653
Fax: 01788 565498

Website: www.crossroads.org.uk
Email: communications@crossroads.org.uk

(Crossroads – Caring for Carers is an umbrella organization. Each of their 205 schemes is an independent charity and a member of Crossroads Association, which is the national body. Their role is to deliver the best quality service for carers to develop new services and reach new carers.)

Estia

Estia Centre
Munro – Guy's Hospital
66 Snowsfields
London SE1 3SS
Tel: 020 7378 3218
Website: www.estiacentre.org

National Association for the Dually Diagnosed (NADD)

Website: www.thenadd.org

NHS DIRECT

Tel: 0845 4647 (24-hour helpline)
Website: www.nhsdirect.nhs.uk

(Directory Online that contains details of many medical conditions, health encyclopaedia, Frequently Asked Questions, Self-Help Guide for Advice, Healthy Living, local services search: dental practices, GP surgeries, opticians, pharmacists, walk-in centres)

The Princess Royal Trust for Carers

Website: www.carers.org
Email: web@carers.org

(The Princess Royal Trust for Carers is incorporated in Scotland as a non-profit-making company. It includes a wide range of information for carers.)

England
142 Minories
London EC3N 1LB
Tel: 020 7480 7788

Scotland
30 George Street
Glasgow G2 1LH
Tel: 0141 221 5066

Valuing People

There is a new Family Carer page on the Valuing People website
Get to it from the 'Help' page.
www.valuingpeople.gov.uk/families.htm

Speech impairment

Afasic
Second Floor
50–52 Great Sutton Street
London EC1V 0DJ
Helpline: 0845 355 5577
Website: www.afasic.org.uk

Learning disabilities

Autism Helpline
Tel: 0870 600 85 85
Email: autismhelpline@nas.org.uk

British Institute of Learning Disabilities (BILD)
Campion House
Green Street
Kidderminster
Worcestershire DY10 1JL
Tel: 01562 723010
Fax: 01562 723029
Website: www.bild.org.uk
Email: enquiries@bild.org.uk

(A not-for-profit organization. It provides information, fact sheets, publications and training and consultancy services for organizations and individuals.)

Down's Syndrome Association
Langdon Down Centre
2a Langdon Park
Teddington TW11 9PS
Tel: 0845 230 0372
Fax: 0845 230 0373
Website: www.dsa-uk.com
Email: info@downs-syndrome.org.uk

Enable
Sixth Floor
Buchanan Street
Glasgow G1 3HL
Tel: 0141 226 4541
Website: www.enable.org.uk

The Foundation for People with Learning Disabilities

Website: www.fpld.org.uk
England
83 Victoria Street
London SW1H 0HW
Tel: 020 7802 0300
Fax: 020 7802 0301
Email: fpld@fpld.org.uk

Scotland
Merchants House
30 George Square
Glasgow
G2 1EG
Tel: 0141 572 0125
Fax: 0141 572 0246
Email: scotland@mhf.org.uk

Mencap

123 Golden Lane
London EC1Y 0RT
Website: www.mencap.org.uk

England
Learning Disabilities Helpline: 0808 808 1111 (free phone)
Email: help@mencap.org.uk

Wales
Learning Disabilities Helpline: 0808 8000 300 (free phone)
Email: wales@mencap.org.uk

National Autistic Society

393 City Road
London EC1V 1NG
Tel: 020 7833 2299
Fax: 020 7833 9666
Email: nas@nas.org.uk
Website: www.nas.org.uk

Mental health problems

The Mental Health Foundation

Website: www.mentalhealth.org.uk

England
83 Victoria Street
London SW1H 0HW
Tel: 020 7535 7400
Fax: 020 7535 7474

Scotland
Fifth Floor
Merchants House
30 George Square
Glasgow G2 1EG
Tel: 0141 572 0125
Fax: 0141 572 0246

African/African-Caribbean people and mental health
Family Health ISIS
183–185 Rushey Green
Catford
London SE6 4BD
Tel: 020 8695 1955
Fax: 020 8695 5600
Email: Fhisis183@btconnect.com

(Advocacy, assertive outreach, counselling, drop-in, creative writing, women's and men's groups, music workshop and gym sessions)

Hearing impairment
National Deaf Children's Society
15 Dufferin Street
London EC1Y 8UR
Tel: 020 7490 8656
Website: www.ndcs.org.uk

Visual impairment
RNIB
105 Judd Street
London WC1H 9NE
Helpline: 0845 766 9999
Website: www.rnib.org.uk

Cerebral palsy

SCOPE
6–10 Market Road
London N7 9PW
Helpline: 0808 800 3333
Website: www.scope.org.uk

Holidays

3H Fund (Help the Handicapped Holiday Fund)
147a Camden Road
Tunbridge Wells TN1 2RA
Tel: 01892 547474
Website: www.3hfund.org.uk
Email: info@3hfund.org.uk

(Group holidays, inclusive of accommodation and transport, for physically disabled people over 11 years old. Volunteers and trained nursing staff provide support. Provide grants to have a UK holiday to families on low income with a physically or mentally disabled dependant.)

Break
Davison House
1 Montague Road
Sheringham NR26 8LN
Tel: 01263 822161
Website: www.break-charity.org
Email: office@break-charity.org

(Has two holiday and short-stay residential care centres in Norfolk. Specializes in holidays for mentally and multiply disabled children and adults, individually or in groups, with or without accompanying parents/staff.)

Calvert Trust

(Purpose-built Centres offering a wide range of sports and recreational activities. Full board or self-catering accommodation.)

Exmoor
Wistlandpound
Kentisbury
Barnstaple EX31 4SJ
Tel: 01598 763221
Website: www.calvert-trust.org.uk/exmoor

Keswick
Little Crosthwaite
Keswick CA12 4QD
Tel: 01768 772254
Website: www.calvert-trust.org.uk/keswick

Kielder
Kielder Water
Hexham NE48 1BS
Tel: 01434 250232
Website: www.calvert-trust.org.uk/kielder

Disabled Holiday Directory
6 Seaview Crescent
Goodwick SA64 0AT
Tel: 01348 875592
Website: www.disabledholidaydirectory.co.uk

(Website directory where you can find or add information on accessible holiday accommodation for people with disabilities)

Family Holiday Association
16 Mortimer Street
London W1T 3JL
Tel: 020 7436 3304.
Website: www.fhaonline.org.uk
Email: info@fhaonline.org.uk

(Provides grants for families in real need of a break for one week's holiday of their choice. The family must be referred to the Association by social services.)

Family Welfare Association
501–505 Kingsland Road
London E8 4AU
Tel: 020 7254 6251
Website: www.fwa.org.uk
Email: fwa.headoffice@fwa.org.uk

(Provides grants for holidays to families with children with disabilities or in need. Applications are considered throughout the year and must be made through a social worker, health visitor or other referring agent.)

Grooms Holidays
PO Box 36
Cowbridge CF71 7GB
Tel: 01446 771311
Website: www.groomsholidays.org.uk

(A non-profit-making charity which offers hotel and self-catering adapted holiday accommodation at approximately half the commercial cost for families with a member with disabilities, or small groups of able-bodied and people with disabilities.)

HELP (Holiday Endeavour for Lone Parents)

57 Owston Road
Carcroft
Doncaster DN6 8DA
Tel: 01302 728791

(Provides low-cost holidays for any lone parent and their children. Needy families, especially those with a disabled child, may be sponsored, funds permitting, usually on the recommendation of a social worker or a doctor.)

Holiday Care

Holiday Care Information Unit
Seventh Floor
Stanley House
4 Bedford Park
Croydon
Surrey CR0 2AP
Tel: 0845 1249971
Website: www.holidaycare.org.uk
Email: holiday.care@virgin.net

(Provides information about all types of holidays for people with special needs, e.g. family holidays, group holidays, activity holidays and holidays for unaccompanied children and young adults. They do not offer financial support. They run a reservation service for accessible accommodation in the UK.)

PHAB England

Summit House
50 Wandle Road
Croydon CR0 1DF
Tel. 020 8667 9443
Email: info@phabengland.org.uk
Website: www.phabengland.org.uk

(National charity working for the integration of people with and without disabilities in the community. Has approximately 500 integrated junior, youth and adult clubs in the UK. Offers holidays and courses, training programmes and an information service.)

Ramblers Association

Second Floor
Camelford House
87–90 Albert Embankment
London SE1 7TW
Tel: 020 7339 8500
Website: www.ramblers.org.uk

(A charity promoting the interests and rights of walkers in the countryside and urban areas. A fact sheet 'Rambling for People with Disabilities' is available.)

Scout Holiday Homes Trust

Gilwell Park
Chingford
London E4 7QW
Tel: 020 8433 7290
Website: www.scoutbase.org.uk/hq/holhomes/index.htm

(Provides inexpensive self-catering holidays at a variety of holiday camps around the UK for any families with a disabled member. They do not have to be a Scout/Guide to benefit.)

Stackpole Trust Centre

Home Farm
Stackpole
Pembroke SA71 5DQ
Tel: 01646 661425

(Provides self-catering, active holidays for families or groups which include people with severe disabilities)

Tripscope

The Vassall Centre
Gill Avenue
Fishponds
Bristol BS16 2QQ
Tel: 0845 758 5641
Website: www.tripscope.org.uk
Email: enquiries@tripscope.org.uk

(Helps solve mobility problems by providing useful information for the planning of journeys by people with disabilities. Information on possibilities for special discounts and concessions on all modes of transport.)

Winged Fellowship Trust

Angel House
20–32 Pentonville Road
London N1 9XD
Tel: 020 7833 2594
Website: www.wft.org.uk
Email: admin@wft.org.uk

(Provides respite for carers and holidays for people with physical disabilities.)

Holiday equipment

British Red Cross

9 Grosvenor Crescent
London SW1X 7EJ
Tel: 020 7235 5454
Website: www.redcross.org.uk
Email: information@redcross.org.uk

(Has a network of medical loan depots, which can lend aids and equipment, including wheelchairs. Details of the nearest depot are available from your local branch of the British Red Cross Society. Some local branches also offer advice about taking a holiday.)

Travel insurance

Travelbility

J & M Insurance Services (UK) plc
14–16 Guilford Street
London WC1N 1DX
Tel: 0207 446 7666
Website: www.jmi.co.uk
Email: jmi@jmi.co.uk

Travelcare Ltd

68 High Street
Chislehurst BR7 5AQ
Tel: 0870 1120085
Website: www.travelcare.co.uk

Appendix

Information from the Mental Health Act (1983)

This appendix is an outline of useful terminology either within the Mental Health Act or as described by the Mental Health Act.

Roles

ASW: Approved Social Worker – a social worker who has had special training on the Mental Health Act

Section 12 Doctor: Approved to apply the Mental Health Act

RMO: Responsible Medical Officer, usually the consultant psychiatrist

Hospital Managers: Hospital board with powers to discharge from hospital

MHRT: Mental Health Review Tribunal

Compulsory admission

Compulsory admission is only possible when the person is suffering from mental disorder, which is split into:

- Mental illness
- Mental impairment
- Severe mental impairment
- Psychopathic disorder

Mental illness

The Mental Health Act does not define mental illness and leaves it as a matter for clinical judgement. People who suffer with mental illness have feelings, thoughts or behaviours which are different from what they normally do and may be unacceptable to themselves and others.

Mental impairment

Mental impairment means 'a state of arrested or incomplete development of mind (not amounting to severe impairment) which includes significant impairment of intelligence and social functioning and is associated with abnormally aggressive or seriously irresponsible conduct'.

Severe mental impairment

Severe mental impairment means 'a state of arrested or incomplete development of mind which includes severe impairment of intelligence and social functioning and is associated with abnormally aggressive or seriously irresponsible conduct'.

This means that under the Mental Health Act (1983) the terms **mental impairment** and **severe mental impairment** may be used to describe people with intellectual disabilities if they present with either:

- Abnormally aggressive behaviour

or

- Seriously irresponsible behaviour

It is recommended that 'no patient should be classified under the Act as mentally impaired or severely mentally impaired without an assessment by a consultant psychiatrist in intellectual disabilities and a formal psychological assessment'. However, in practice this does not always happen.

Psychopathic disorder

Psychopathic disorder means 'a persistent disorder or disability of mind (whether or not including significant impairment of intelligence) which results in abnormally aggressive or seriously irresponsible conduct'.

People with certain forms of personality disorder could be detained under this category.

Short term orders

These are concerned with **admission for assessment** when the person does not give consent. They can apply to any mental disorder, which does not need to be specified. They include: Sections 2, 4, 5 (2), 5 (4), 135 (1), 135 (2) and 136.

Section 2 (admission for assessment)

- Preferable to have consent for treatment, but not necessary

- Application by an Approved Social Worker (ASW) or nearest relative
- Two medical recommendations required (one must know the person)
- Lasts for 28 days

The person admitted can apply to the Mental Health Review Tribunal against detention within the first 14 days of the detention.

Section 4 (emergency admission for assessment)

- Used in emergency situations only
- Application by Approved Social Worker (ASW) or nearest relative
- One medical recommendation (preferably by someone who has previous knowledge of the person) required
- Only the Registered Medical Doctor (RMO) can discharge the person
- No right of appeal
- Must have consent for treatment

Section 5 (2) (report on hospital inpatient)

- For the detention of an informal patient (i.e. a person previously willing to be in hospital), in emergency situations
- Can be detained for up to 72 hours
- One medical recommendation required
- Must have consent for treatment
- Only an RMO can discharge the patient
- No right of appeal

Section 5 (4) (nurses' six hour holding power)

- For the detention of an informal (voluntary) patient, who is already being treated for mental disorder in the hospital and now wants to leave
- The nurse must be a 'First Level Qualified Nurse' in mental illness or intellectual disabilities
- Must have consent for treatment
- Must see a doctor as soon as possible

Section 135 (1) and 135 (2) (warrant to search and remove patients)

Section 135 (1) allows an Approved Social Worker (ASW) to seek a warrant from a court to enter a locked premises if there is cause to suspect that the person is suffering from mental disorder and has been ill treated, neglected or not kept under proper control or is living alone and is unable to care for themselves.

Section 135 (2) allows the retaking of detained patients who have gone absent without leave.

A police officer or staff officer from the hospital can apply to the magistrates' court to authorize police entry to the private premises.

Section 136 (mentally disordered persons found in public places)

A police officer may remove a person to a place of safety if the person appears to be in immediate need of care or control and the police officer thinks it is necessary to do so in the person's interest or for the protection of others. A doctor and an Approved Social Worker (ASW) must see the person within 72 hours. Places of safety include psychiatric hospital, police station, and social services residential accommodation or mental nursing home.

Long term orders

These orders are concerned with **admission for treatment** (Sections 3 and 7). The type of mental disorder must be specified.

Section 3 (admission for treatment)

- Application by nearest relative or an Approved Social Worker (ASW)

- Two medical recommendations are needed

- Lasts for up to six months; they are renewable for another six months, then annually

- May be discharged by the RMO, hospital managers, Mental Health Review Tribunal (MHRT) or nearest relative (but must apply to the hospital managers)

- Medication may be given for first three months without consent if required

- An RMO may grant leave of absence

- The person may appeal to the Mental Health Act managers when the order is being renewed. The person may appeal to the MHRT once during the first six months, once during the second six months if it is renewed, and then once a year if it is further renewed

- A Section 3 order cannot normally be imposed if the nearest relative objects

Section 7 (application for guardianship)

This section exists to enable patients to receive care in the community where it cannot be provided without the use of compulsory powers. It provides an authoritative framework for working with the patient, with a minimum of constraint, to achieve as independent a life as possible within the community. Where it is used it must be part of the patient's overall care and treatment plan.

ASSESSMENT AND APPLICATION FOR GUARDIANSHIP

Approved Social Workers (ASW) and doctors should consider guardianship as a possible alternative to admission to, or continuing care in, hospital.

An application for guardianship should be accompanied by a comprehensive care plan established on the basis of multi-disciplinary discussions.

GROUNDS FOR GUARDIANSHIP

- The person is over the age of 16 years
- The person is suffering from a mental disorder
- The person requires guardianship in the interests of the welfare of that person or for the protection of others
- The applicant for guardianship is either the nearest relative or ASW to the local Social Services
- The application is based on two medical recommendations (one MHA approved doctor)

The order lasts initially for six months and is then renewable for a further six months and then for a year at a time. The Responsible Medical Officer is responsible for renewing the order.

POWERS OF GUARDIAN

- To require the person to live at a place specified by the guardian
- To require the person to attend at specified places for medical treatment, occupation, education or training

- To require access to the person be given at the person's residence to people outlined in the Mental Health Act (e.g. ASW)

Guardianship does not provide legal authority to physically detain someone in accommodation. The individual's consent is required for any form of treatment. The guardian can be any individual or social services authority. The person has the right of appeal to the Mental Health Review Tribunal. The RMO, social services and nearest relative can discharge the order at any time.

Orders associated with criminal proceedings

- Section 35 – to prepare a report on a person's mental condition as an alternative to custody. Lasts for up to 28 days
- Section 36 – for sentenced prisoners to be remanded to hospital for treatment
- Section 37 – admission of an offender to hospital for treatment
- Section 38 – detention in hospital for a convicted person who has not yet been sentenced
- Section 41 – Home Office restriction order

Resources

HyperGuide: Mental Health Act
Website: www.hyperguide.co.uk/mha/index.htm
(Provides a basic guide to mental health law – the Mental Act 1983)

Mental Health Act Commission (England and Wales)
Second Floor
Maid Marian House
56 Hounds Gate
Nottingham NG1 6BG
Tel: 0115 943 7100
Website: www.mhac.trent.nhs.uk

(Investigates complaints about treatment from anyone who has been detained under the Mental Health Act)

Mental Health Foundation
Website: www.mentalhealth.org.uk
(Information on existing legislation and fact sheets available)

England
Seventh Floor
83 Victoria Street
London SW1 0HW
Tel: 020 7802 0300
Email: mhf@mhf.org.uk

Scotland
Fifth Floor
Merchants House
30 George Square
Glasgow G2 1EG
Tel: 0141 572 0125
Email: Scotland@mhf.org.uk

National Alliance of the Relatives of the Mentallly Ill (NARMI)

Tydehams Oaks
Tydehams
Newbury
Berkshire RG14 6JT
Tel: 01635 551923 (Answerphone service – all calls retruned the same day)

(Was formed in 1992 by careers as a campaign organization, but now provides advocacy, advice, medical information and information about Government legisaltion)

Further Reading and Resources

American Psychiatric Association (1994) *Diagnostic and Statistical Manual of Mental Disorders. Fourth edition.* Washington, DC: American Psychiatric Association Press.

Andrews, G. and Jenkins, R. (eds) (1999) *Management of Mental Disorders (UK Edition).* Sydney: World Health Organisation Collaborating Centre for Mental Health and Substance Abuse.

Attwood, T. (2001) *Asperger's Syndrome: A Guide for Parents and Professionals.* London: Jessica Kingsley Publishers.

Bouras, N. (ed) (1999) *Psychiatric and Behavioural Disorders in Developmental Disabilities and Mental Retardation.* Cambridge: Cambridge University Press.

Bouras, N. and Holt, G. (eds) (1997) *Mental Health in Learning Disabilities Training Package.* London: Pavilion Publishing.

Bouras, N., Holt, G., Day, K. and Dosen, A. (eds) (1999) *Mental Health in Mental Retardation: The ABC for Mental Health, Primary Care and Other Professionals.* World Psychiatric Association Section of Mental Retardation. Available online at www.wpanet.org/home.html

Brayne, H. and Martin, G. (1999) *Law for Social Workers.* Sixth Edition. London: Stanley Thomes Publishers.

British Institute of Learning Disabilities (in preparation) *Dementia Resource Pack and Booklets on Dementia for People with Learning Disabilities.* Kidderminster: British Institute of Learning Disabilities.

Carnaby, S. (ed) (2002) *Learning Disability Today.* London: Pavilion.

Davidson, G.C. and Neal, J.M. (1996) *Abnormal Psychology.* New York: John Wiley and Sons, Inc.

Department of Health and the Department of Education and Skills (2002) *BILD Easy Guide to Physical Interventions.* London: Department of Health.

Emerson, E. (1995) *Challenging Behaviour: Analysis and Intervention in People with Learning Disabilities.* Cambridge: Cambridge University Press.

Foundation for People with Learning Disabilities (2002) *Count Us In: The Report of the Committee Inquiry into Meeting the Mental Health Needs of Young People with Learning Disabilities.* London: Foundation for People with Learning Disabilities.

Harris, J. (1995) *Developmental Neuropsychiatry.* Oxford: Oxford University Press.

Harris, J., Allen, D., Cornick, M., Jefferson, A. and Mills, R. (1996) *Physical Interventions – A Policy Framework.* London: British Institute of Learning Disabilities.

Holt, G. and Bouras, N. (eds) (1997) *Mental Health in Learning Disabilities Handbook.* London: Pavilion Publishing.

Holt, G. and Bouras, N. (eds) (2003) *Autism and Related Disorders: The Basic Handbook for Mental Health, Primary Care and Other Professionals, World Psychiatric Association.* London: Section of Psychiatry of Mental Retardation.

Jones, G., Jordan, R. and Morgan, H. (2001) *All About Autistic Spectrum Disorders – A Booklet for Parents and Carers.* London: The Mental Health Foundation.

Joyce, T., Ditchfield, H. and Harris, P. (2001) 'Challenging behaviour in community settings.' *Journal of Intellectual Disability 45*, 2, 130–138.

La Vigna, G. and Donnellan, A. (1986) *Alternatives to Punishment: Solving Behaviour Problems with Non-aversive Strategies.* New York: Irvington.

Mencap (2002) *The Housing Timebomb.* London: Mencap.

Nind, M. and Hewett, D. (2001) *A Practical Guide to Intensive Interaction.* Kidderminster: BILD Publications.

Ramsay, R., Gerada, C., Mars, S. and Szmukler, G. (eds) (2001) *Mental Illness: A Handbook for Carers.* London: Jessica Kingsley Publishers.

Royal College of Psychiatrists (2001) *DC-LD Diagnostic Criteria for Psychiatric Disorders for Use with Adults with Learning Disabilities.* London: Gaskell.

Social Services Inspectorate (2000) www.bild.org.uk/factsheets/direct_payments.htm

The Mental Health Foundation (2002) *Today and Tomorrow: The Report of the Growing Older with Learning Disabilities Programme.* London: The Mental Health Foundation.

World Health Organisation Collaborating Centre for Research and Training for Mental Health (eds) (2000) *WHO Guide to Mental Health in Primary Care.* London: Royal Society of Medicine Press.

'Valuing People: A New Strategy for the Twenty-First Century.' Department of Health (2001)

'A National Service Framework for Mental Health.' Department of Health (1999)

Acts

Carers Act (1996)

Carers (Recognition and Services) Act (1995)

Disability Discrimination Act (1995)

Mental Health Act (1983)

The Human Rights Act (2000)

Websites

www.autism.org
Centre for the Study of Autism

www.bild.org.uk
British Institute of Learning Disabilities (BILD)

www.bps.org.uk
British Psychology Society

www.cot.co.uk
College of Occupational Therapists

www.dh.gov.uk
Department of Health

www.dh.gov.uk/policyandguidance/healthandsocialcaretopics/mentalhealth/fs/en
Department of Health: Mental Health

www.dsa-uk.com
Down's Syndrome Association

www.epilepsynse.org.uk
The National Society for Epilepsy (NSE)

www.epilepsy.org/uk
Epilepsy Action

www.estiacentre.org
Estia Centre

www.fpld.org.uk
Foundation for People with Learning Disabilities

www.homeoffice.gov.uk
Home Office

www.hyperguide.co.uk/mha/index.htm
Guide to the Mental Health Act

www.mencap.org.uk
MENCAP

www.mentalhealthcare.org.uk
Maudsley NHS Trust and the Institute of Psychiatry

www.mentalhealth.org.uk
Mental Health Foundation

www.nas.org.uk
National Autistic Society

www.nhsdirect.nhs.uk
NHS Direct

www.rcn.org.uk
Royal College of Nursing

www.rcpsych.ac.uk
Royal College of Psychiatrists

www.rcstl.org
Royal College of Speech and Language Therapists

www.valuingpeople.gov.uk
Valuing People Support Team

www.valuingpeople.gov.uk/families.htm
Valuing People (Carer's web page)

Glossary

Mary Jane Spiller

Acute
This is used to describe an illness when it has a sudden beginning, and it often lasts for a short amount of time.

Alzheimer's disease
A form of dementia that gradually gets worse, and is irreversible. There is an overall impairment of intelligence, memory and personality.

Anti-epileptic medication
Also known as anticonvulsants. These drugs are used to treat epilepsy.

Anxiety disorders
A group of mental illnesses where the sufferer has an exaggerated normal reaction to stressful events. Severe anxiety is the main disturbance.

Assessment
This involves the appraisal of a situation or problem. Examples of assessments include psychiatric assessments and functional assessments.

Autism
A condition that is characterized by delay and unusual development of social relationships, verbal and non-verbal communication and imagination. A person with autism has a restricted range of activities and interests.

Behavioural techniques
Methods used to modify someone's behaviour and actions. Examples can include 'shaping' and 'modelling'. In behavioural therapy people are encouraged to learn new ways of behaving through gradual changes.

Biological intervention
A drug-based intervention.

Bipolar disorder or Bipolar affective disorder
The term used for people who experience depressive, manic or mixed affective episodes at different times. It is also known as **Manic depression**.

Braille
A touch-based writing and reading system. Patterns of raised dots represent letters and numbers.

Care plan (management care plan)
A written document that identifies the health and social care needed by someone with a mental illness, and who will provide this.

Care Programme Approach (CPA)
A framework for providing care for someone with a mental illness, introduced in 1991, to ensure the community services involved, such as health services, social services, social security and housing, are co-ordinated and work together. It involves the assessment of an individual's health and social needs, and the development of a care plan, and the appointment of a care co-ordinator. There are two levels of CPA: Standard and Enhanced.

Challenging behaviour
Behaviour that people think is abnormal or unusual within the person's culture. It is seen as a problem because of what it can do to the person involved and others around them.

Clinical psychologist
A clinical psychologist is a professional who aims to reduce psychological distress and to promote and enhance psychological well-being. They work with people with mental or physical health problems of all ages. They are trained in different types of psychological interventions and counselling.

Cognitive behavioural therapy (CBT)
A therapy based on the idea that the way you think about things (your cognition) has an effect on the way you feel. Behavioural techniques are also used to gradually change the way you think about something.

Counselling
When someone has counselling they spend time talking to a professional counsellor. They discuss their problems and feelings, and the counsellor can give sympathetic and objective help. This advice is usually practical, and they work together to manage difficult life events such as the loss of someone close, past and present relationships, mental health issues and disorders.

Dementia
Dementia is a progressive decline in mental ability. Memory, thinking and problem-solving ability, concentration and perception all gradually get worse over time. It is usually age-related. There are different types. The most common is Alzheimer's disease.

Depression
A mental disorder in which the sufferer has a persistent feeling of low mood, changes in sleep pattern, low self-esteem, and a lack of motivation.

Disorder
Mental illnesses are also called mental disorders.

Down syndrome
A syndrome that is caused by a genetic condition. People with Down syndrome have lower IQs and slower development than their peers, and they have particular physical characteristics, such as big tongues.

Emotional disorders
Disorders in which a mood or feeling such as fear or anxiety are central to the mental health problem.

Epilepsy
A tendency to have repeated seizures that originate in the brain.

Intervention
This is a general term used for any procedure or technique designed to change something, such as a mental illness or challenging behaviour. Interventions can be biological, psychological or social.

Learning disabilities
'Learning disabilities' is a term used in the UK to describe people who have difficulties understanding and learning new things (a significant impairment of intellectual functioning). They also have difficulties in communication, self-care, and awareness of health and safety (a significant impairment of adaptive/social functioning). These difficulties or impairments are present from childhood, and are not the result of an accident or an adult illness. People are often described as having **mild**, **moderate** or **severe** learning or intellectual disabilities. These labels are linked to IQ test scores.

Manic depression
A mood disorder. At times sufferers have feelings of depression (low and sad) and at other times feelings of mania (elated, excited and over-confident). Also known as **Bipolar disorder** or **Bipolar affective disorder**.

Mental health problems
This covers a wide range of problems, from the everyday worries and grief we experience, to serious problems that can interfere with someone's ability to cope on a day-to-day basis.

Mental illness
Severe mental health problems. It is a controversial term as there is no universally agreed cut-off point for it and the label is highly stigmatizing.

Multi-agency involvement
Professionals from many different areas are involved in the same case, for example from different areas of health and social services.

Multi-disciplinary team (MDT)
Team made up of professionals from different backgrounds, such as from psychology, psychiatry, speech and language therapy, and occupational therapy.

Neuroses
A group of disorders in which the sufferer has an exaggerated form of a normal reaction to stressful events. There are no hallucinations or delusions.

Occupational therapy / Occupational therapist
Assesses how the individual's mental health problems affect their ability to do everyday things. They work out interventions to maximize the person's ability to do things and their independence.

Person-centred planning (PCP)
Person-centred planning is a way of helping people to work out what they want, for now and for the future, the support they might need, and then helping them to get it. It is a continual process of listening and learning that places the individual in the centre. It is of central importance in the White Paper 'Valuing People'.

Psychiatric assessment / Mental health assessment
This is an evaluation of a psychiatric problem that takes into account the physical, psychological and social components.

Psychiatric disorder
A psychiatric disorder is a significant behavioural or psychological problem that can cause someone severe distress, or prevent them from coping in everyday situations. A psychiatric disorder is not an expected response to a traumatic event such as grieving the loss of a loved one. It also does not include behaviour that some people might see as abnormal for religious, sexual or political reasons.

Psychological
This refers to the mind and the various processes that go on within it, such as thoughts, feelings and memories, and the way we behave as a result.

Psychological intervention
There are many different types such as counselling, cognitive behavioural therapy (CBT) and psychotherapy.

Psychological theories
These are explanations for something, which are based on aspects of the mind such as thoughts, feelings or memories.

Psychoses
A group of disorders in which the sufferer is unable to recognize reality and hallucinations and delusions can occur. A sufferer may be unaware of his or her own mental condition.

Psychosocial problems
These have both a psychological and social basis.

Psychotherapy
A form of therapy that tries to understand someone's current problems by looking at their past experiences.

Schizophrenia
A group of psychiatric disorders characterized by disordered thinking, hallucinations, false beliefs that are unusual for the person's cultural and educational background, unusual behaviour and withdrawing from everyday life.

Sensory disorder
A problem with one or more sense, such as sight, hearing, touch, taste or smell.

Side effects
Unwanted effects of medication.

Social intervention
An intervention that aims to reduce the suffering caused by an illness, or to make it more manageable, through changing aspects of a person's social situation. They include improving a person's living situation, or changing their daytime activities.

Social network
The group of people someone interacts with.

Statutory services
These are services that the government legally has to provide, such as education for children under 16.

Therapeutic intervention
Any form of treatment, such as medication, counselling or moving to improved accommodation, which aims to cure an illness or at least reduce the suffering and make it more manageable.

Therapies
See **Intervention**.

Transition plan
This involves planning for when a young person with intellectual disabilities leaves school, which starts from the age of 14. These plans look at where the person will live, what they will do in the daytime etc.

White Paper 'Valuing People'
This is a document produced by the Government in 2001. It is the first White Paper on learning disabilities for 30 years. It sets out proposals for improving services for people with intellectual disabilities. These are based on four key principles:

- Civil rights
- Independence
- Choice
- Inclusion

The proposals will lead to improvements in education, social services, health, employment, housing and support for people with intellectual disabilities and their families and carers.

About the Authors

Nick Bouras is Professor of Psychiatry at the Institute of Psychiatry, London and Consultant Psychiatrist at South London and the Maudsley NHS Trust. He is editor of the journal *Intellectual Disability Research - Mental Health* and has published extensively in community psychiatry and mental health aspects of people with intellectual disabilities. He is the editor of *Mental Health in Mental Retardation: Recent Advances and Practices (1994), Psychiatric and Behavioural Disorders in Developmental Disabilities and Mental Retardation (1999).*

Anastasia Gratsa is a psychologist at the Estia Centre, Institute of Psychiatry, London. She has extensive experience in research and psychotherapy and is a former manager of a residential care home/therapeutic community.

Steve Hardy is the Training Co-ordinator at the Estia Centre. He is a Registered Nurse in Learning Disabilities and has a MSc in Mental Health and Learning Disabilities. His interests include mental health promotion, service user involvement, staff training and accessible information for people with learning disabilities. He is also a citizen advocate.

Geraldine Holt is Consultant Psychiatrist in Learning Disabilities at South London and the Maudsley NHS Trust and Honorary Senior Lecturer at the Institute of Psychiatry, London. She is a fellow of the Royal College of Psychiatrists and currently senior policy Adviser at the Department of Health. She has published widely on the subject of mental health and learning disabilities and she is co-editor of *Mental Health in Learning Disabilities Training Package (1997).*

Theresa Joyce is Head of Psychology for Adults with Learning Disabilities Services at the South London & Maudsley NHS Trust. She has published on a range of issues, including service quality, challenging behaviour and on responses to abuse. Current interests include mental capacity and consent, as well as the use of Cognitive Behavioural Therapy (CBT) as an intervention for a range of mental health needs.

Mary Jane Spiller is a researcher at the Estia Centre. She is a psychology graduate from the University of Bath. She has a broad range of research experience in psychology and mental health in services, and has spent some time working as a research assistant in the USA, at Harvard University. She is actively interested in increasing service user and carer participation in health service research.

Index

233

blood tests 28, 37
 and medication use 122,
 124, 127, 190
 for thyroid function 67
'Books Beyond Words' series
 30, 39
boredom 34
Braille 138–9
brain chemicals 24, 118, 120,
 121, 125, 146
brain surgery 193
Break 211
breast screening 37
breathing exercises 133
British Association for
 Counselling and
 Psychotherapy 64
British Confederation of
 Psychotherapists (BCP)
 128
British Institute of Learning
 Disabilities (BILD) 68,
 139, 160, 162, 164,
 165, 208
British Psychological Society
 (BPS) 108, 128
British Red Cross 214–15
British Sign Language 138–9
bulimia 72, 130
buspirone (Buspar) 127

caffeine 48, 60
Caldwell, Phoebe 139
Calvert Trust 211–12
carbamazepine (Tegretol) 123,
 191
care co-ordinators 86, 87, 91
care managers 101, 102
 and advocacy 104
 and carers 200, 204, 205
 as part of Community
 Learning Disability
 Teams 94, 95
 and respite services 106
care plans, holistic 28–9, 91
Care Programme Approach
 (CPA) 82–3, 86–8, 91,
 156
 enhanced 87
 standard 86–7
care staff 200

care workers 200
carers
 assessments for 197–8, 200,
 201–3, 204
 confidentiality issues 155
 coping 115, 198–9
 employment 205
 general advice for 29–33
 information 13–15, 17–18,
 20
 legislation 68, 200, 201
 and the National Carers
 Strategy 203–4
 and the National Service
 Framework for Mental
 Health 201
 needs and support 12, 17,
 20, 197–215
 organizations 31, 38, 70,
 206
 self-help 198, 205–6
 services for 200–1, 203
 and therapeutic
 interventions 114, 139
 types 199–200
Carer's Act (1996) 201
Carers Association of Ireland
 38
Carers Grant 205
Carers Line 38, 70
Carers National Association 38,
 70
Carers Online (Part of Carers
 UK) 206
Carers (Recognition and
 Services) Act (1995) 68,
 200
Caring for Carers 203–4
Centre for Eating Disorders,
 Scotland 74–5
Centre for the Study of Autism
 182
cerebral palsy 211
challenging behaviour 10, 16,
 141–51
 and abuse 146
 Antecedent Behaviour
 Consequences
 approach to 145,
 149–50
 of autism 178–9
 consent issues 142, 151

contextual influences on
 145–6, 150
 definition 23, 141, 142–3
 of depression 47
 environmental influences on
 145, 148, 150
 explanations of 143–7
 functional analysis of 142,
 147–50
 functions/purposes of
 141–2, 143–7
 individual influences on
 145
 and physical illness/pain
 146
 prevalence 143
 reinforcers of 144–5, 146,
 148, 150
 therapeutic interventions
 132, 142, 150–1,
 178–9
 triggers 146
 see also difficult behaviour
challenging behaviour workers
 94, 97
challenging needs practitioners
 98
Chartered Psychologists 128
Chartered Society of
 Physiotherapy 108
check-ups 36–7
chewing, excessive 72
Chinese Mental Health
 Association 38
chlorpromazine (Largactil) 118,
 122, 124
cholinesterase inhibitors
 (Aricept, Exelon,
 Reminyl) 128
Circles Network UK 108
CITA 78
Citizens Advice Bureau 165–6
cleanliness, compulsive 61
clinical psychologists 90, 91–2,
 94, 96, 98
clonazepam (Rivotril) 127
clozapine (Clozaril) 124
cluster housing 106
cognitive behavioural therapy
 (CBT) 92, 98, 128,
 129–30
cognitive functioning 187